THE
IMAGINED
CITY

THE IMAGINED CITY

San Francisco in the Minds of Its Writers

by John van der Zee and Boyd Jacobson
with biographical sketches by Julie Smith
and a bibliography compiled by Sayre Van Young

A CALIFORNIA LIVING BOOK

Published in cooperation with Friends of the San Francisco Public Library

This book is expanded and adapted from an exhibition created by John van der Zee and Boyd Jacobson for the Friends of the San Francisco Public Library.

— *The Editors*

Since this copyright page cannot accommodate all acknowledgments, they are to be found on the following two pages.

Adams, Alice. Excerpt from *Families and Survivors*. Copyright © 1974 by Alice Adams. Reprinted by permission of the author and Alfred A. Knopf, Inc.

Angelou, Maya. Excerpt from *I Know Why the Caged Bird Sings*. Copyright © 1969 by Maya Angelou. Reprinted by permission of Random House.

Asher, Don. Excerpt from *The Piano Sport*. Copyright © 1966 by Don Asher. Reprinted by permission of the author and Atheneum.

Atherton, Gertrude. Excerpt from *Ancestors*. Copyright © 1907 by Harper & Brothers. Reprinted by permission of Harper & Row.

Bierce, Ambrose. Excerpt from *The Ambrose Bierce Satanic Reader:* Selections from the Invective Journals of Ambrose Bierce compiled and edited by Ernest Jerome Hopkins. Copyright © 1968 by Ernest Jerome Hopkins. Reprinted by permission of Doubleday & Company, Inc.

Brautigan, Richard. Excerpt from *Trout Fishing in America*. Copyright © 1967 by Richard Brautigan. Reprinted by permission of Delacorte Press/Seymour Lawrence.

Bryant, Dorothy. Excerpt, with changes by author, from *Miss Giardino*. Copyright © 1978 by Ata Books. Reprinted by permission of the author.

Busch, Niven. Excerpt from *California Street*. Copyright © 1959 by Niven Busch. Reprinted by permission of Simon & Schuster.

Caen, Herb. Excerpt from *Only in San Francisco*. Copyright © 1960 by Herb Caen. Reprinted by permission of Doubleday & Company, Inc.

Acknowledgments

Photo Credits

(First listing is credit for author's photo, second listing is credit for text photo.)

Adams
San Francisco Examiner/Lee Romero
Hal Lauritzen

Angelou
Marlene Callahan Wallace/Courtesy Random House
San Francisco Public Library

Asher
San Francisco Examiner/Fran Ortiz
San Francisco Examiner

Atherton
Courtesy, The Bancroft Library
California Historical Society

Bierce
Courtesy, The Bancroft Library
California Historical Society

Brautigan
Erik Weber/Courtesy Delacorte Press/Seymour Lawrence
San Francisco Examiner

Bryant
Photo by Jane Scherr/Courtesy the author
Hal Lauritzen

Busch
Barbara Hall/Courtesy the author
Gabriel Moulin Studios

Caen
Courtesy the author
California Historical Society

Carpenter
© 1979 by Grace Warnecke
San Francisco Public Library

Connell
Ann Ashley/Copyright 1980
California Historical Society

Dana
Courtesy, The Bancroft Library
California Historical Society

Ferlinghetti
San Francisco Examiner/Paul Glines
San Francisco Public Library

Forbes
San Francisco Examiner
California Historical Society

Gaines
San Francisco Examiner/Fran Ortiz
Jerry Stoll

George
Courtesy, The Bancroft Library
California Historical Society

Gold
San Francisco Examiner/Judith Calson
San Francisco Examiner

Hammett
San Francisco Public Library
San Francisco Public Library

Harte
Courtesy, The Bancroft Library
San Francisco Maritime Museum

Hinckle
Vici MacDonald
San Francisco Examiner

Hoffer
Andree L. Abecassis/Courtesy Harper & Row
California Historical Society

Holdredge
©Russell Leake/Courtesy the author
California Historical Society

Kerouac
Robert Frank/Courtesy Viking Press
Jerry Stoll

Kroeber
University of California Press
Lowie Museum of Anthropology, University of California, Berkeley

Lee
San Francisco Examiner
California Historical Society

Leffland
Courtesy the author
San Francisco Examiner/Lee Romero

Lewis
Courtesy, The Bancroft Library
California Historical Society

London
California Historical Society
California Historical Society

Norris, F.
Courtesy, The Bancroft Library
Gabriel Moulin Studios

Norris, K.
Courtesy, The Bancroft Library
California Historical Society

Olsen
San Francisco Examiner/Bob McLeod
California Historical Society

Royce
Courtesy, The Bancroft Library
California Historical Society

Saroyan
Courtesy Creative Arts Book Company
San Francisco Public Library

Sterling
Courtesy, The Bancroft Library
California Historical Society

Stevenson
San Francisco Examiner
California Historical Society

Stewart
Cecil Davis/Courtesy the author
California Historical Society

Twain
Courtesy, Mark Twain Papers, The Bancroft Library
San Francisco Public Library

Contents

Introduction

On the November day in 1978 when San Francisco Mayor George Moscone and Supervisor Harvey Milk were murdered, I was in a jury box on the fourth floor of the City Hall. The courtroom, where the news had arrived in dismaying increments — sirens, cleared hallways, sealed doors, rumors, and finally an official announcement by a shaken court reporter — was the one in which my father had once sat as judge. As a boy, I had sat in that room to await the outcome of similar crimes, anticipating the verdict of people like me who sat in judgment in that same jury box. I had come full circle.

For a week, we attempted to carry on the functions of justice in the atmosphere of a giant funeral home: twin biers and flanked floral displays in the rotunda, ant-lines of mourners, security searches at every door, eulogies and protests on the front steps. Over everything fell the vast, recriminatory gloom of compound civic tragedy: first, Jim Jones, late of San Francisco, the prophet of assembly-line martyrdom in Jonestown, Guyana, and then, less than two weeks later, the shootings.

Self-reproach, under such circumstances, takes on a certain romantic glow. One's city has become important, if only as the momentary gathering place of humankind's more malevolent impulses, and so, by association, has oneself. One feels the tug of twin temptation: to withdraw into one's own affairs, dissociating oneself from this city and all cities as doomed, antiquated life forms, or to accept the widespread condemnation of an entire community as final — to subside, rather than perservere.

I withdrew into the work that underlies this book: the insulated order of library stacks, the modest discoveries of photographic archives. And what did I come upon, in politeness and scholarship? — the very passions and turmoil of the city I had fled.

Josiah Royce's analysis of the mental effects of stress on men of the gold rush revealed not only the tortured eyes of the wrecked human being behind the stock comic figure of Emperor Norton but the curiously bland, stoic face of the cop-fireman-supervisor-assassin, Dan White. In the political scheming of the union-exploiter Abe Ruef was a flash-forward to the political scheming of a racial exploiter, Rev. Jim Jones. Bad as things were in San Francisco, did they truly match the year-in, year-out, murder-a-night barbarity of the Barbary Coast?

"Anyone who advocates an open town," said my father, who, as a Western Union boy, had delivered telegrams in a downtown San Francisco with a whorehouse on nearly every block, "never lived in one."

What I deplored in the city I lived in could be found, in slightly altered, frequently romanticized form, in every aspect of that city's history. That San Francisco is — and always has been. And we have tried to reveal it through the selections in this book.

But another San Francisco emerged as well. It is a work of the imagination, not just of one writer but of the many writers, poets, and dramatists who have lived and worked in San Francisco and have fashioned the city in the process of their work. This compound, imaginative San Francisco serves as a kind of reservoir of potentialities, and it is as real, as enduring, as the stone-and-steel city we experience each day.

An example: In researching the quote from Frank Norris, Boyd Jacobson and I sorted through photographs of the city of that day, of the mansions and wharves and hotels and banks and narrow, winding, European-style byways. How little of the works of serious men and women of affairs — financiers and railroad builders and politicians — has survived! And yet Frank Norris's work is alive and whole, in touch with living people through a book in a library. Whose work was really serious? Who truly built to last?

Something else is revealed when photographs are matched with works of the imagination: they don't really fit. And in the differences between photograph and text, we begin to sense something of the imagination's mysteries. We feel the writer's ability to take what is around him or her and transform it into story, legend, myth. We discover Izzy Gomez, saloon-keeper and local character, the raw material from which Willam Saroyan fashioned the enduring figure of Nick, the bartender in *The Time of Your Life*. Or Dashiell Hammett's Sam Spade, matched with pictures of cops from the San Francisco Hammett inhabited. In the disparity between what we see and what is said — the mysterious currents of feelings, emotion, invention — something of the tidal pull of imagination itself comes clear. It is all the stronger because we can't quite quantify it, can't put our finger on it.

In assembling such a collection, one can't help but be struck by the professional competence and variety of contemporary San Francisco writing. Perhaps because that writing is done independently, following no movement, cult, or school, energies that would otherwise have been turned outward are concentrated on the work. Whatever the reason, little doubt remains that more writing of value is coming out of San Francisco now than in several of the city's well-publicized Golden Ages. If San

Francisco now depends less than in the past on its writers as a tourist attraction, San Francisco writers also rely less on the city for protective cover. Good San Francisco writers would be good anywhere.

My one regret in completing this book is that the work of some good writers has been omitted. I can only plead ignorance and the limits of time and space, and suggest to the overlooked writers that I am among them — while offering the consolations of posterity. If history tells us anything, it is that the writer of this time and place who will be remembered best is one who labors now in obscurity.

I would like to express my gratitude to Boyd Jacobson, my friend and partner, whose eye and instinct have brought this idea to life; to San Francisco's Friends of the Library, who sponsored the exhibit upon which this book is based; and, for the photographs and research upon which we relied, to Laverne Dicker of the California Historical Society, Tom Moulin of Moulin Studios, Pat Akre of the San Francisco Main Library, John Maounis of the San Francisco Maritime Museum, Jerry Stoll, and to The Bancroft Library, University of California, Berkeley.

And to the people at California Living Books — Leslie Carr, who brought all the parts and pieces of this book into a whole, and Hal Silverman and David Charlsen, who felt this work deserved to end up back where it all began: in the company of books.

— J.v.d.Z.

The Writers and
Their Imagined City

Alice Adams

A Southerner by birth, Alice Adams (1926—   ) frequently sets her books in San Francisco simply, as she puts it, "because I live here. I don't see that San Francisco needs any boosting from me." Yet her San Francisco scenes are so vivid that Patricia Holt wrote in a review of Adam's *Listening to Billie:* "It is, first of all, a terrific book for San Franciscans because the characters are forever roaming and rendezvousing all over town, in Huntington Park and Potrero Hill and the lower Mission and upper Grant, and in hideaway places at Stinson Beach, Big Sur, and Mendocino."

When she searches her memory, Adams herself recalls that "a friend once said of my first novel, 'that's the kind of really neurotic love affair that could happen only in San Francisco'." Adams says she isn't sure what the friend meant; she herself is from Fredericksburg, Viriginia.

A graduate of Radcliffe, Adams supported herself with a succession of office jobs, including those of secretary, clerk, and bookkeeper, while she waited for the world to realize she was a writer. Magazines noticed first: the *New Yorker, Atlantic Monthly, Redbook, McCall's,* and *Paris Review.*

Careless Love, the tale of the neurotic love affair, was published in 1966. In 1974, *Families and Survivors* was released. It was followed by *Listening to Billie* and a collection of short stories called *Beautiful Girl.*

Rich Rewards is scheduled for publication late in 1980. "It's about a young woman who spends a year — and only a year — in San Francisco," says Adams. She encounters "love, murder, and crazy weather."

The house, a Victorian mansion, has been scheduled for destruction. It was bought by an extremely successful Italian builder, who is a distant cousin of the mayor's. Here, in an elegant neighborhood, on a block with a stupendous view of the Bay and Marin County, the builder will put yet another high-rise, apartments for which he can charge exalted rents. The kids are allowed to rent the house from month to month, for what comes to around fifty dollars apiece;
there are quite a few of them. (It is not, strictly speaking, a commune — just friends living in the same house.)
This arrangement came about because one of the kids is the son of a lawyer who is close to the mayor, and who is also a friend of the builder's. It makes everyone, including the mayor, feel pleasantly tolerant;
they are being nice to hippies.

Alice Adams,
FAMILIES AND SURVIVORS

Maya Angelou

When Maya Angelou (1928–) was three, she was sent by her divorced parents to live with relatives in Arkansas. She later recorded some of the hardships of being a black child in the South in *I Know Why the Caged Bird Sings,* the first volume of her autobiography.

Moving to San Francisco in her teens, she became the first black female fare collector for the city's Municipal Railway. Her tenacity and determination, helped along by talent in several crucial areas, have made her "first black female" many times since then — most notably the first to write a screenplay that became a movie (*Georgia, Georgia*), in 1972.

While still in her teens, Angelou studied dance and drama. During the 1950s, when North Beach was a place of cabarets and coffeehouses, she sang and danced at the Purple Onion and soon became one of the city's most popular performers.

With the beginning of her nightclub career, the misfortunes of her childhood seemed suddenly to reverse themselves. On the same day she was cast in a Broadway musical, she was offered a part in a touring production of *Porgy and Bess.* She took the tour job and, when she returned, everything she touched continued to turn gold.

As her career blossomed, so did her political consciousness. She served as coordinator for Dr. Martin Luther King's Southern Christian Leadership Conference and later went to Africa for several years. During the 1960s, Angelou wrote plays and poetry; in 1970, *I Know Why the Caged Bird Sings* was published. Since then, several more volumes of her autobiography and her poetry have followed, along with more plays and screenplays.

"The majority of writers from San Francisco," says Angelou, "are white. They see romance in San Francisco which really includes people of other races only as exotics. I also see romance, but since I'm black I have written about the city from my point of view."

I was given blood tests, aptitude tests, physical coordination tests, and Rorschachs, then on a blissful day I was hired as the first Negro on the San Francisco streetcars.

Mother gave me the money to have my blue serge suit tailored and I learned to fill out work cards, operate the money changer and punch transfers. The time crowded together and at an End of Days I was swinging on the back of the rackety trolley, smiling sweetly and persuading my charges to "step forward in the car, please."

For one whole semester, the streetcars and I shimmied up and scooted down the sheer hills of San Francisco. I lost some of my need for the Black ghetto's shielding-sponge quality, as I clanged and cleared my way down Market Street with its honky-tonk homes for homeless sailors, past the quiet retreat of Golden Gate Park and along closed undwelled-in-looking dwellings of the Sunset District.

Maya Angelou,
I KNOW WHY THE CAGED
BIRD SINGS

Don Asher

A book by Don Asher (1926–   ) is likely to be about musicians and inclined to be set in San Francisco, where Asher has lived and played piano for the past twenty years.

Born in Worcester, Massachusetts, Asher is the son of a chemist and was educated to be one himself. He received bachelor's and master's degrees from Cornell University and actually worked as a research chemist for about a year. But being a jazz pianist proved more to his liking, so Asher chucked science in favor of music.

He also chucked the East Coast in favor of San Francisco, where he is a familiar bush-haired presence in saloons and salons alike. For years, while he was becoming a writer, he supported himself with his music, working as house pianist in the early 1960s at the famous hungry i in North Beach.

His first book, *The Piano Sport*, was published in 1966. Many of the San Francisco scenes in that book and in Asher's others take place in North Beach — a North Beach that no longer exists.

"I would like to think," says Asher, "that my books about entertainers and musicians captured some of the flavor of the North Beach night club district before the era of the nudes and shills, when the coffeehouses mingled in friendly fashion with family restaurants, cabarets and jazz clubs."

In 1975, *Raise Up Off Me*, a book he did with Hampton Hawes, won the ASCAP-Deems Taylor Award. He has written six other books, including *The Piano Sport* and has a passion beyond music and writing — tennis.

After work we went to Enrico's for coffee. Broadway was in flux, white coated parking attendants jumping, traffic backed up and horns blasting while the crowds poured from the Jazz Workshop, El Matador, Burp Hollow, Finocchio's. . . . A half-dozen beatniks passed our sidewalk table, the girls looking temptingly dissolute and carnal with their accentuated eyes and dark lank hair. The loose black woolen sweaters and black stockings made me think of Hester . . . *to conceal my charms man!*

"Look at that stuff," Norman said, digging into his cheesecake. "Forget the Beats, they wash twice year — college girls, secretaries, baby; airline hostesses . . . And the ones with date are mostly squares!"

Don Asher,
THE PIANO SPORT

Gertrude Atherton

Born in San Francisco, Gertrude Atherton (1857–1948) was sent East to school, but her education was cut short. "I should have remained two years," she wrote in her eighty-fourth year, "but absent-mindedly got engaged to two young men at once and thought California was the safest place for me. Soon after my arrival home I married George Henry Bowen Atherton . . ."

Reputedly, marriage made her miserable, and the report is borne out by the fact that in many of her novels talented young heroines break their domestic bonds to pursue independence. Atherton herself was released by the untimely but obliging death of her husband in his thirties.

She immediately left her daughter with relatives and went to New York. Though she was already a published writer locally, she wanted a national forum for the novels she was eventually to write — sixty of them, many of which were set in San Francisco.

Gertrude Atherton's San Francisco, wrote Kevin Starr, "embodied a myth . . . of spacious possibilities and defiant high style. . . . And yet (the myth) also contained within itself its own contradictions; the city could be shabby and treacherous, promising more than it could deliver. Her ambivalence drove her to nearly half a lifetime of expatriation."

Although she often portrayed heroines who felt imprisoned by the city's isolation and smugness, in the late 1920s Atherton herself moved back to spend her final years in San Francisco.

She was quite vocal about the "rejuvenation" treatments she took in Vienna in 1923, and it was generally agreed that she seemed stunningly youthful in her last quarter century.

In those years, before she died at ninety-one, she lived with her daughter on Green Street, serving on city commissions by day and conducting a glittering salon by night.

There are hundreds of my sort. You've seen them at the real Bohemian restaurants; young men mad with life and the sense of their own powers; all of them writing, painting, composing, editing — mostly talking. Then at other tables the old-young men who have shrugged their shoulders and simmered down like myself; lucky if they haven't taken to drink or drugs to drown regrets. Still other tables — the young-old men, quite happy, and generally drunk. Businessmen and some professionals are the only ones that forge steadily ahead; with precious few exceptions. But you don't see them often in the cheap Bohemian restaurants, which have a glamour for the young, and are a financial necessity for the failures. Never was such a high percentage of brains in one city. But they must get out. And if they don't go young they don't go at all. San Francisco is a disease.

Gertrude Atherton,
ANCESTORS

Ambrose Bierce

At the time of his greatest influence, Ambrose Bierce (1842–1914 [?]) was known as "the wickedest man in San Francisco." With a single stroke of his pen he could make or break a reputation — literary, political, or otherwise. And since Bierce had a poor opinion of his fellow human and a devilish gift for satire, he was more feared than loved. But he was much admired. For no matter how vicious, his invective was brilliantly crafted, and he was a colorful eccentric in a city that adored such things.

A humble nightwatchman and refugee from Ohio, he began writing a satirical column called the "Town Crier" for the San Francisco *News Letter* and was soon its editor. He also wrote scary stories for the *Overland Monthly* and was a member of the same literary clique as Bret Harte and Mark Twain.

In 1871, he went to England, but came back five years later. For the next ten years he wrote his merciless and influential "Prattler" column for the *Argonaut,* also contibuting to the *Wasp* and eventually becoming its editor. But his true heyday as San Francisco's literary czar began in 1887, when William Randolph Hearst took over the *San Francisco Examiner* and prevailed upon Bierce to be that paper's "Prattler."

Bierce ruled imperiously and unchallenged until December 1896, when he suddenly received a telegram from Hearst ordering him to leave immediately for Washington. The telegram bade him stop Congress from passing a railroad refunding bill. Bierce did not hesitate. Displaying theretofore unsuspected talents for investigative reporting, he stopped the bill almost single-handedly.

After that he wrote for the *American* and *Cosmopolitan,* but by then his influence had waned, and so had his talent. He lived in Washington until 1913 when he returned to California on his way to Mexico. He was last heard from in 1914. No one knows when or how he died.

M r. Charles Crocker (says the telegraph) has
purchased a handsome residence in New York.
He deserves the very handsomest residence
in America for the patience and truly Christian fortitude
with which he has long endured the most hideous.
There are uglier buildings in America than the Crocker
house on Nob Hill, but they were built with public
money for a public purpose; among the
architectural triumphs of private fortune and
personal taste it is peerless. If Mr. Crocker
doesn't want it any more, I'd
like to burn it down.

Ambrose Bierce,
THE AMBROSE BIERCE
SATANIC READER

Richard Brautigan

At seventeen, Richard Brautigan (1935–   ) decided to be a writer; at twenty-five, he wrote his best-known book, *Trout Fishing in America.* He spent the interval "learning to write a sentence."

He studied the mysteries of the sentence in a way few novelists would have chosen — by writing several volumes of poetry. And then, continuing what he once called "my lonely direction of writing like a timber wolf slipping quietly through the woods," he invented his own form for novels and short stories.

After the late 1960s, when his books began to be widely circulated, Brautigan inched his way from cult popularity to mainstream and critical acceptance.

"San Francisco," he says, "is the only city I could ever have come to on the planet to be stimulated and encouraged to write the books that I have written.

"I came to San Francisco in the middle '50s as a young man and now, on January 24, 1980, as these words are being written, I'm a middle-aged man. My writing grew up in this city."

Brautigan himself grew up in Washington, Oregon, and Montana, and never attended college. He has a daughter, Ianthe Elizabeth. Brautigan has written eight novels, nine books of poetry, and a book of short stories. He divides his life among San Francisco, Montana, and Japan.

Those facts about his life are virtually the only ones that Brautigan acknowledges publicly. Though friendly and accessible, he is an intensely private man.

"It's really something," he once wrote, "to have fame put its feathery crowbar under your rock, and then upward to the light release you, along with seven grubs and a sow bug."

I remember Trout Fishing in America Shorty passed out in Washington Square, right in front of the Benjamin Franklin statue. He had fallen face first out of his wheelchair and just lay there without moving.

Snoring loudly.

Above him were the metal works of Benjamin Franklin like a clock, hat in hand.

A friend and I got to talking about Trout Fishing in America Shorty one afternoon. We decided the best thing to do with him was to pack him in a big shipping crate with a couple of cases of sweet wine and send him to Nelson Algren.

Nelson Algren is always writing about Railroad Shorty, a hero of *The Neon Wilderness* (the reason for "The Face on the Barroom Floor"), and the destroyer of Dove Linkhorn in *A Walk on the Wild Side.*

We thought that Nelson Algren would make the perfect custodian for Trout Fishing in America Shorty. Maybe a museum might be started. Trout Fishing in America Shorty could be the first piece in an important collection.

We would nail him up in a packing crate with a big label on it.

CONTENTS:
    Trout Fishing in America Shorty
OCCUPATION:
    wino
ADDRESS:
    c/o Nelson Algren
    Chicago

Richard Brautigan,
TROUT FISHING IN AMERICA

Dorothy Bryant

Dorothy Bryant (1939–   ) is a rarity — a native San Franciscan. The daughter of a mechanic and a bookkeeper, she grew up in the Mission District, an area she later used as a backdrop for her novel, *Miss Giardino.*

"I think that's unusual," she says. "Most novels and movies about San Francisco use the regular repertoire of the Golden Gate Bridge, a couple of winding hills, maybe a little North Beach.

"Up until recently the Mission District was simply a very unfashionable part of San Francisco. Now it's becoming too expensive for the working class. When I lived there, everyone's ambition was to move over Twin Peaks to other areas. I don't know of anything else that's been written that gets deeply into that area as an important neighborhood, out of which came an enormous number of people who did many things and went other places."

Bryant herself went to Berkeley, where she lives and writes fulltime, after a 23-year career as a schoolteacher in San Francisco and later in the East Bay.

Bryant is the author of a number of novels, most of which were first published by her own press, Ata Books, as well as a nonfiction work titled *Writing a Novel. The Kin of Ata Are Waiting For You,* a utopian novel, is perhaps her most widely known work.

When she first began to write, she says, she felt lonely. Other writers seemed to feel that "whatever happened had to be happening in the East. And then all of a sudden the place was full of writers. I think it's one of the most important things that's happened in San Francisco in the last ten or fifteen years."

Her broad, golden face was nearly unlined, and her long black hair was thick, but she must have been nearly as old as Anna. Polynesian? Indian? Probably some mixture, like so many of the people in The Mission.

Anna remembered how the superintendent had offered her "... Senior English out at Lowell High. You've earned it after twenty years of ..."

"Oh, no, thank you, no," she had told him. "I would miss the Mission faces."

Dorothy Bryant,
MISS GIARDINO

Niven Busch

By the time Niven Busch (1903–   ) left boarding school, his work had been published in several magazines. When he was forced to leave Princeton for lack of funds, he landed a job with *Time* magazine. "Of course," he points out, "a cousin of mine was the editor. I have always advised young writers in beginning their career to make sure they have a cousin who is the editor of a national publication."

Nepotism or no, Busch prospered at *Time* and soon became associated with the *New Yorker* as well, kissing both magazines good-bye in 1931 to accept a job as a writer for Warner Brothers Pictures, Inc. For eight years he turned out one screenplay after another until, in 1939, he wrote his first novel, *The Carrington Incident*. After that, he divided his time between the two forms.

He has written some thirty movies, so many of them psychological horse operas that the *Village Voice* recently said, "We credit Niven Busch, King Vidor and Raoul Walsh as the creators of the modern western."

Busch now lives and works in San Francisco, which he has used liberally as a backdrop in five of his twelve novels: *Day of the Conquerors, California Street, The San Franciscans, The Gentleman from California,* and *Continent's End,* about a family that gets rich in oil.

"I think you could almost say that of all living authors, I've written the most about San Francisco," says Busch. "To me it has always appeared a fantastically exciting city both for the past, always somehow present in the air, and for its momentous present — its proximity to world events. It's 'the place where things happen,' as one of its authors said, and I think that's why I've written so much about it."

"Where are the clipper ships? What's happened to them!" Fabian demanded. He capered in front of Anchylus, glaring at him accusingly. As usual when in an orating mood, he went on without waiting for an answer.

"Grand creatures, like birds, those ships. Hauled in the gold hunters. Hauled in the pianos, the whores, furniture and pickaxes, my boy, and the Chinamen; those ships changed this burg from a tenth-rate Spanish outpost to what you see today. The lovely ships! Where have they gone now? Can you tell me that?"

Niven Busch,
CALIFORNIA STREET

Herb Caen

Like it or not (he says he doesn't), Herb Caen (1916–) is "Mr. San Francisco" to readers of his daily gossip column in the *San Francisco Chronicle*. In the 1940s he gave the name to a character he had invented for his column. People thought he was writing about himself and, to his discomfort, applied the tag to him. "It has a rah-rah quality I don't like."

Yet if ever San Francisco had a booster, it's Caen, the leader of the "don't-call-it-Frisco" movement, the author of ten books and uncountable magazine articles on the city, and the inventor of the sly phrase, "Baghdad-by-the-Bay."

Caen also contributed the word "beatnik" to the language, but he insists that isn't his greatest achievement: "I was prouder of calling the Bay Bridge the 'Car-Strangled Spanner'."

For all that, Caen isn't a native. Born and raised in Sacramento, he began his snooping career with a high school gossip column under the pseudonym "Raisin Caen."

He grew up to be a police reporter for the *Sacramento Union* and moved to his adopted city in 1936 to become the *Chronicle's* radio columnist. He started slipping newsy items into the column and made it a hit. But because radio was a competing medium, the *Chronicle* decided to drop the column two years after Caen got it. Faced with unemployment, he sold his publishers the idea of a local interest column. It first ran on July 5, 1938. Caen was lured to the *San Francisco Examiner* for a brief eight year stint in the 1950s but went back to his typewriter at the *Chronicle* on 1958.

"The secret of Caen's success," a fellow newsman once said, "is his outstanding ability to take a wisp of fog, a chance phrase overheard in an elevator, a happy child on a cable car, a deb in a tizzy over a social reversal, a family in distress and give each circumstance the magic touch that makes a reader an understanding eyewitness of the day's happenings."

(49) 5949 Busy Market Street of the City of the Golden Gate, San Francisco, California. Copyright 1901 by Underwood & Underwood.

The day before: Old San Francisco — "the gayest, lightest-hearted, most pleasure-loving city of the Western continent" — died in the dawn of April 18, 1906. The day before, in the memory of those who survive, had been unforgettably brilliant. Spring was in the air and all San Francisco, poised unknowingly on the brink of chaos, was dizzy with pleasure. A modern column-about-town, written on that day, might have read something like this:

IN ONE EAR: Young John Barrymore, appearing here in Richard Harding Davis's new play, *The Dictator* (fair), is asking for trouble; or is his big romance with the fiancée of that Venetian-glass collector just another of his Tall Tales? . . . Bullock & Jones, the fancy tailors, are slapping a $465 suit on Wilson Mizner for a long-unpaid clothing bill; now that he's married to the rich Mrs. Charles Yerkes, you'd think the overdressed slob would pay up . . . Wondering muse: Does Mayor Eugene Schmitz know about the big crap game going on nightly in the basement of the new City Hall? Does he care? . . .

Herb Caen,
"The Day Before," ONLY IN SAN FRANCISCO

Don Carpenter

Don Carpenter (1931–   ) grew up watching the lights of San Francisco from his home in the Berkeley hills. "To me," he says, "that's what San Francisco has always been — what you see from Berkeley. It's goddam magnificent. It's always been heaven to me. To come to San Francisco and to write about San Francisco — that's like heaven. Ask any Berkeley boy."

When Carpenter grew up, he put heaven, particularly the North Beach sector of it, in his work, which he began at age sixteen. He wrote short stories, fragments, plays, and paragraphs throughout high school, college at Portland State, four years in the air force, and a return to school to get a master's degree at San Francisco State.

Then he hung out his shingle as a writer, publishing his first novel, *Hard Rain Falling,* in 1966. When *Blade of Light* came out the next year, one critic said, "He stands among new American novelists of the 1960s gifted with conscience and destined for literature."

Two more books followed and then the film script for *Payday.* After *The True Life Story of Jody McKeegan* was published in 1975, there followed a long period of silence.

During that period Carpenter "spent a lot of time writing failed motion pictures — twelve of them." Finally, because he had a contract to write a book about Hollywood and couldn't write about it while working there, he quit.

"I love San Francisco, and I cleave to San Francisco and I believe in her," he says. "I will never write for Hollywood again."

Carpenter lives in Mill Valley. His latest book, *A Couple of Comedians,* was published in January 1980.

Well, he would fling it in their teeth. He drank off about half the pint, jammed the bottle into his hip pocket, and took off for Market Street. When he left his room he was angry, and determined to make trouble, but by the time he got down to Market he felt just fine and sauntered along with the early evening crowd, savoring the pure freedom of it, the way people all dressed differently, the way the women looked and smelled, the way the streetcars sounded, the glitter of the lights, the strange exciting music from the hotdog joints, the corniness of it all, the cheapness. The vulgarity which is vulgar only if you haven't been away for such a long time and in a place so dull as prison.

Don Carpenter,
HARD RAIN FALLING

Evan Connell

Evan Connell (1924—) lives in Sausalito and collects Pre-Columbian art, as does the hero of his novel, *The Connoisseur.* He has once or twice been seen at Sausalito's no name bar, a groggery suspiciously similar to the Po-Po Club, the locale of Connell's series of short stories about two characters named Leon and Bébert.

Only one of his twelve books, *The Diary of a Rapist,* is actually set in San Francisco. "I like living here. I've been here a long time," he says. "But I haven't really employed the Bay Area as a setting. I don't really know if there's a San Francisco school of writing or not. When people talk about the 'California school' or the 'Chicago school,' I rather think that's something dreamed up by critics rather than the people themselves."

One of the San Francisco Bay Area's most distinguished writers, Connell is so noted for his insightful characterization that a writer for the *New Republic* said he is "like a character actor who disappears into his role . . ."

Connell is a native of Kansas City, Missouri. He sampled higher education at a smorgasbord of schools that included Dartmouth, the University of Kansas, Stanford, and Columbia. From 1943 to 1945, he served as a navy pilot.

In 1953, he was a Eugene Saxton Fellow and ten years later a Guggenheim Fellow. In 1967, he received a Rockefeller Foundation grant.

Locally Connell is known as an extremely taciturn man of conservative appearance, eminently polite and likeable.

After that? Along Pacific Heights, downhill to the Marina & sat on a bench for an hour or so watching ships coast under the bridge. Thought about experiences I've had, also reflected on things I should have done but was afraid to do. It's apparent I'm not getting much out of my life. But of course on the other hand I ought to consider myself extremely fortunate what with no serious financial problems, secure job, etc. For example, there I was enjoying my freedom in sight of those prisoners on Alcatraz. Were any of them looking across the water at me? What were they thinking? Probably that they'd give anything to be where I was.

Evan Connell,
THE DIARY OF A RAPIST

Richard Henry Dana

Born in Cambridge, Massachusetts, Richard Henry Dana, Jr. (1815–1882), was the son of a poet and essayist. He enrolled in Harvard but nearly lost his sight when he got the measles in his junior year.

To regain his health, he shipped out as a common sailor before the mast on the brig *Pilgrim*. He kept a minute diary of the *Pilgrim*'s progress around Cape Horn to California, published in 1840 as *Two Years Before the Mast*.

The voyage did indeed restore his health, and the book earned him his place in literature. It focused public attention on the brutal treatment of sailors, and its vivid descriptions of California and its early settlers also aroused interest in what was then a Spanish colony.

Dana did not stay in the West however. He re-entered Harvard, was graduated at the head of his class, and became a lawyer. He helped to found the Free Soil Party, which preceded the Republican Party, and sometimes acted as an attorney for runaway slaves.

From 1861 to 1866, he was United States Attorney for Massachusetts and later served in the Massachusetts legislature. Despite his identification with the plight of sailors and other downtrodden folk, Dana was said to have a remote and arrogant manner that forestalled true success in politics. Though he ran for Congress, he was not elected and when he won a presidential appointment as minister to England, the Senate failed to confirm it.

In his later years, he became an authority on international law, specializing in admiralty law, and wrote another book. *The Seaman's Friend* came to be a standard authority on naval law both in this country and in England.

About thirty miles from the mouth of the bay, and on the south east side, is a high point, upon which the presidio is built. Behind this point is the little harbour, or bight, called Yerba Buena, in which trading vessels anchor, and, near it, the Mission of Dolores. There was no other habitation on this side of the bay, except a shanty of rough boards put up by a man named Richardson, who was doing a little trading between the vessels and the Indians.

Richard Henry Dana,
TWO YEARS BEFORE THE MAST

Lawrence Ferlinghetti

After the horrible deaths of nine hundred People's Temple members, and then of a San Francisco mayor and supervisor in November 1978, the *San Francisco Examiner* commissioned Lawrence Ferlinghetti (1919–) to write "a poem of hope" for the city. With the publication of "An Elegy to Dispel Gloom," the newspaper declared that "despite the lack of any official title, Lawrence Ferlinghetti is San Francisco's poet laureate."

In the 1950s Ferlinghetti was an important spokesman for the beat generation and a leader of the poetry revival of the period. But his own poetry was barely the beginning of his cultural contribution.

When he and his partner, Peter Dean Martin, opened City Lights bookstore in 1953, they opened what Ferlinghetti himself called "a center for the intellectual community." They also invented a new literary institution — the paperback bookstore.

Then, in 1955, when City Lights began publishing books, Ferlinghetti gave his fellow beats an outlet, a voice beyond poetry readings in dingy churches. The poet and his partner were charged with publishing obscene material after they brought out Allen Ginsberg's *Howl,* and the resulting trial received minute media examination. The charges were dismissed, Ferlinghetti and company came out as the good guys, and San Francisco's prestige as a focus of literature was vastly uplifted.

In the 1960s, Ferlinghetti was active in the anti-war movement and, as what he called "a bridge figure" between the beats and the hippies, continued to be a spokesman for the culturally disaffected.

Asked in a recent interview why he came to San Francisco, Ferlinghetti admitted, "I used to make up all kinds of literary reasons for coming here . . . but I've been thinking about it recently and I suppose one of the biggest reasons . . . was that San Francisco was the only big city in the United States near a wine-growing area. . . ."

And the great Chinese dragon has eaten a hundred humans
and their legs pop out of his underside
and are his walking legs which are
not mentioned in the official printed
program in which he is written up as
the Great Golden Dragon made in
Hong Kong to the specifications of the
Chinese Chamber of Commerce and
he represents the force and mystery of
life and his head sways in the sky
between the balconies as he comes
followed by six Chinese boy scouts
wearing Keds and carrying strings of
batteries that light up the dragon like
a nighttime freeway . . .

Lawrence Ferlinghetti, "The Great Chinese Dragon,"
    from STARTING FROM SAN FRANCISCO

Kathryn Forbes

Kathryn Forbes (1909–1966), who created the loveable characters of *I Remember Mama*, was also Kathryn Anderson McLean of Burlingame.

When her book, *Mama's Bank Account*, became first a play and then a movie (both called *I Remember Mama*) and later a television series ("Mama"), a local columnist wrote: "The scene is San Francisco and the time is the wonderful (in retrospect) years following the fire — but the story of Mama is universal and timeless."

Forbes spent her own early years in post-earthquake San Francisco, and her grandmother, like "Mama," was a Norwegian immigrant. The book is based on reminiscences of those days, and the author was fond of quoting an aunt who remarked, "It's a very nice book, Kathryn, but I don't see what all the shouting's about. Anyone in the family could have written it."

For years Forbes collected rejection slips. In the mid-1930s, she started to write radio scripts — free — for a local station. NBC liked her stories and began to pay her $75 apiece for them, but the network wanted her to move to Hollywood. She refused and returned to short story writing.

Three more years passed before she made her next sale — to a Canadian magazine — for $35. She sent her next effort, a nostalgic tale of her childhood, to *Reader's Digest*. The magazine paid her $750 and two months later printed a second installment. Thousands of readers wrote in demanding more "Mama" stories.

So Forbes wrote *Mama's Bank Account*.

Published in 1943, it was an instant best seller. Forbes had no further trouble selling her stories.

And if anyone ever asked us where we were born, Mama instructed us, we should say "San Francisco." Didn't copies of our birth certificates, neatly framed and hung on the wall of Papa's and Mama's room, testify to that proud fact?

"After all," Papa used to tease her, "after all, San Francisco isn't the *world*."

But to Mama it was just that. The world.

Kathryn Forbes,
MAMA'S BANK ACCOUNT

Ernest J. Gaines

Opinions vary about Ernest J. Gaines (1933–). Some say he is a Southern writer who happens to live in San Francisco; others feel that he is a San Francisco writer who merely uses the South as subject matter. The only reason anyone cares is that everyone wants to claim him, for agreement is universal on Gaines's distinction as a writer. For instance: In 1958, he won a Wallace Stegner Fellowship; in 1959, the San Francisco Foundation's Joseph Henry Jackson Award; in 1966, a grant from the National Endowment for the Arts; and in 1972, awards from the Commonwealth Club of California, the Louisiana Library Association, and the Black Academy of Arts and Letters.

His work is frequently compared to that of William Faulkner, and his best-known book, *The Autobiography of Miss Jane Pittman,* has been called "the embodiment of the black experience in America."

"All of the six books I've had published have been set in Louisiana," says Gaines. "But we have the most beautiful city in the world, so why not live here? I don't have to sit in the middle of the ocean to write about what the water looks like."

A native of Oscar, Louisiana, Gaines moved to Vallejo at age fifteen. He served in the army from 1953 to 1955 and after that earned his bachelor's degree from San Francisco State. He went back for further study at Stanford and in 1971 served as writer-in-residence at Denison University in Granville, Ohio.

"I've tried to write about San Francisco, but others seem to do it so much better," says Gaines. "I've got to get rid of the Louisiana thing, and maybe someday I can concentrate on California."

It had happened suddenly. It had sneaked up on him. No, no it had not. It had only come less directly than it had in the South. He was not told that he could not come into the restaurant to eat. But when he did come inside, he was not served as promptly and with the same courtesy as were the others. When he went into a store to buy a pair of pants or a pair of socks, he was treated in the same manner as he had been in the restaurant. And when he and his parents were looking in the papers for another place to rent, he remembered how his mother's finger made an imprint under each place that said "colored" when all the time there were other places which she would have preferred living in and which were much cheaper. The imprint under that one word, because it was made in San Francisco, would be imprinted on his mind the rest of his life.

Ernest J. Gaines,
CATHERINE CARMIER

Henry George

In 1858, after arriving too late for the gold rush along the Fraser River in Canada, Henry George (1839–1897) came to San Francisco dead broke. He was to stay nearly twenty years, finally leaving as a world-famous economic philosopher.

Born in Philadelphia, George quit school at fourteen, worked as a clerk for two years, and then shipped out to Australia and India. After that he took time out to learn typesetting and then signed up as steward on the *Shubruck,* the ship he eventually left to find gold in Canada.

When he came to San Francisco without so much as a flake of the stuff, he fell back on typesetting — and in those days it was a small leap from printing to journalism. George worked for eight years as a typesetter and then for five years as an editor for several newspapers, including the *San Francisco Chronicle.*

In 1871, with two partners, he started his own paper. But the *San Francisco Daily Evening Post* failed four years later.

By this time, George had spent several years as heavily involved in Democratic party politics as he was in his work, even making an unsuccessful bid for the state assembly. When he found himself at loose ends after his paper failed, the Democratic governor gave him a job — as state inspector of gas meters.

He held the job for three years — until a Republican became governor — and during this period wrote his most famous book, *Progress and Poverty,* published in 1879. The book, with its "single tax" theory, caught the spirit of discontent in a country emerging from a depression.

George, an instant success, moved to New York in 1880 to continue his writing and lecturing career. He lived there the rest of his life, running twice for mayor. Four days before the election that was to decide his second attempt, he was killed by a stroke.

The Farallone Islands, off the Bay of San Francisco, are a hatching ground of sea-fowl, and a company who claim these islands employ men in the proper season to collect the eggs. They might employ these men for a proportion of the eggs they gather, as is done in the whale fishery, and probably would do so if there were much uncertainty attending the business; but as the fowl are plentiful and tame, and about so many eggs can be gathered by so much labor, they find it more convenient to pay their men fixed wages. The men go out and remain on the islands, gathering the eggs and bringing them to a landing, whence, at intervals of a few days, they are taken in a small vessel to San Francisco and sold. When the season is over the men return and are paid their stipulated wages in coin. Does not this transaction amount to the same thing as if, instead of being paid in coin, the stipulated wages were paid in an equivalent of the eggs gathered? Does not the coin represent the eggs, by the sale of which it was obtained, and are not these wages as much the product of the labor for which they are paid as the eggs would be in the possession of a man who gathered them for himself without the intervention of any employer?

Henry George,
PROGRESS AND POVERTY

Herbert Gold

Herbert Gold (1924–   ), a Clevelander by birth, has set nearly a quarter of his eighteen books in San Francisco, his adopted city, which he calls "the last traditional metropolitan village."

"It's a kind of maxi-family for people who live alone," he explains. "I don't have to drive my car more than once every two or three days. I can get almost everywhere by walking or bus. If I'm lonely I can go to Just Desserts, Enrico's, or the Washington Square Bar and Grill and meet someone to talk with. And if I don't meet anyone, I can go to City Lights and find something to read."

Gold believes San Francisco is "the last city like that." He likes to compare it with the Paris of his student days and the Greenwich Village of his early writing years. Working from time to time as a college teacher, Gold has lived in a number of American cities, as well as Haiti and Paris.

Throughout his writing career, which began in 1951 with *Birth of a Hero,* Gold has frequently been a critical success and the recipient of awards and honors.

He has held Fulbright, Hudson Review, Guggenheim, and Ford Foundation fellowships. He has also received an Inter-American Cultural Relations Grant to Haiti, an Ohioana Book Award, a Longview Award, and a grant from the National Institute of Arts and Letters.

Besides his novels, Gold has written short stories, essays, and magazine articles too numerous to mention — perhaps even to count — and several screenplays.

"You never wanted a quieter way? You could have had a quieter life, Dad."

The question seemed to stop him suddenly. He looked out over the glistening blue-and-white, watery and green, jeweled city of San Francisco which I had chosen for my own. We had talked about trade with China, but there was no trade with China; I had explained about the miners settling here, but the mines were mostly shut now, and the fortunes tamed. He liked brawling cities, and had no taste for this sweet air off the ocean, unbreathed by lungs, factories, smokestacks.

Herbert Gold,
FATHERS

Dashiell Hammett

Dashiell Hammett (1894–1961) was "not the typical San Francisco writer," noted Warren Hinckle in *San Francisco City* magazine. "For one thing, he became successful. For another . . . he didn't just use the town as a setting: San Francisco was a character in Hammett's work, at times a hood, at times a madam, at times the tough beautiful crust of the earth that influenced people and defined the course of events in his world of low life with high class insights of a compact beauty."

Hammett, the founder of hard-boiled detective fiction, lived in San Francisco for eight years. For a year he worked as an operative for the Pinkerton National Detective Agency. In 1921, he quit in order to write, but the rejection slips poured in, and he was forced to find work again.

So, from 1922 to 1927, he banged out advertising copy for Albert S. Samuels Jewelers. His relationship with Samuels is legendary, for the jeweler was more patron than employer. Under his wing, Hammett wrote thirty-two stories for *Black Mask* magazine.

In 1927, the first installment of *Red Harvest,* Hammett's first novel, was published in *Black Mask.* The book was a critical success.

The Thin Man, considered by many to be a poor example of Hammett's work, was his most successful novel. By the time he wrote it, Hammett was much like its hero, Nick Charles — wealthy, alcoholic, and losing interest in his work. After 1934, when it was published, he no longer wrote books. He worked as a screenwriter, a script doctor, and occasional book reviewer.

He also became politically active and may have joined the Communist party. He was jailed for six months in 1951 after he refused to testify before the New York State Supreme Court about his politics. When he died ten years later, his companion, Lillian Hellman, said, ". . . he seemed to me a great man."

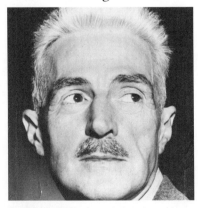

Spade turned from the parapet and walked up Bush Street to the alley where men were grouped. A uniformed policeman chewing gum under an enameled sign that said *Burritt St.* in white against dark blue put out an arm and asked:

"What do you want here?"

"I'm Sam Spade. Tom Polhaus phoned me."

"Sure you are." The policeman's arm went down. "I didn't know you at first. Well, they're back down there," he jerked a thumb over his shoulder. "Bad business."

"Bad enough," Spade agreed, and went up the alley.

Dashiell Hammett,
THE MALTESE FALCON

Bret Harte

At five, Bret Harte (1836–1902) parodied his primer; at six, he was reading Shakespeare. At eleven, he published a poem in the *New York Sunday Atlas.* His career then took a ten-year downward slide.

Young Harte left school in New York to work in a lawyer's office and then in a counting house. In 1854, he came to California, where he was a teacher, a miner, a drugstore clerk, a journalist, and a printer.

In 1857, he was setting type for the literary magazine *Golden Era* when an editor spotted his talent and offered him a dollar a column. So Harte went back into the writing business in San Francisco.

His first collection of poems, *The Lost Galleon and Other Tales,* and his satirical *Condensed Novels* were published in the late 1860s. In 1868 he became the first editor of a new San Francisco magazine called the *Overland Monthly,* which published his most famous stories — "The Luck of Roaring Camp" and "The Outcasts of Poker Flat." The *Overland* also published a comic verse narrative called "Plain Language from Truthful James," which made a bit of a splash in the literary East. In 1870, Harte was made professor of recent literature at the University of California.

The next year, with tempting offers in the East, Harte crossed the continent to make his fortune. But the offers, including a contract to write for the *Atlantic Monthly,* failed to pan out. Harte fell upon such hard times it was rumored he paid bills with stamps enclosed in autograph requests.

A novel, *Gabriel Conroy,* and a play, *Ah Sin,* written with Mark Twain, were unsuccessful.

Hart was bailed out by Uncle Sam — he got a job as United States consul, first in Prussia, then in Scotland. He became a favorite in European literary circles and eventually moved to London, where he was able to make his living writing.

He died of throat cancer in the spring of 1902.

I can recall myself at such times wandering along the City Front, as the business part of San Francisco was then known. Here the lights were burning all night, the first streaks of dawn finding the merchants still at their counting-house desks. I remember the dim lines of warehouses lining the insecure wharves of rotten piles, half filled in, that had ceased to be wharves, but had not yet become streets — their treacherous yawning depths, with the uncertain gleam of tarlike mud below, at times still vocal with the lap and gurgle of the tide. I remembered the weird stories of disappearing men found afterward imbedded in the ooze in which they had fallen and gasped their life away.

Bret Harte, "Bohemian Days in San Francisco"
from THE WRITINGS OF BRET HARTE

Warren Hinckle

Though some complain that his prose is as florid as his Irish mug, no one denies that Warren Hinckle (1938—   ) writes as passionately about San Francisco as anyone of his generation — possibly of his century.

In "Hinckle's Journal," his column in the *San Francisco Chronicle,* he keeps his readers abreast of the events — usually the mishaps and miseries — in the lives of the least fortunate of their fellow citizens. Hinckle's subjects are more often than not denizens of the Mission District, frequently Irish, and always set upon by those who wish them ill — usually landlords.

Hinckle began the most important phase of his journalistic career on the *Chronicle* in 1962 but left two years later to become editor of *Ramparts* magazine. He turned *Ramparts* into the leading muckraking journal of its day and later tried to keep up the good work in *Scanlan's Monthly,* which lasted from 1969 to 1972 and never quite caught the popular fancy. In 1975, he edited the splashy but short-lived *City* magazine and finally went back to the *Chronicle.*

Hinckle received the Tom Paine Award in 1967 for work in exposing the CIA's infiltration in this country, and he is the author of several books and numerous magazine pieces. The *Washington Post* called him an editorial genius; *New York* magazine called him "a rascal of national stature." Throughout nearly two decades on the San Francisco literary scene, Hinckle has loomed somewhat larger than life on the cityscape, always doing rather more than his part to uphold the tradition of the roughneck-eccentric gentleman of letters. His trademark eyepatch and black patent dancing slippers are as familiar to patrons of the city's most sordid dramshops as they are to Hinckle's friends in lace-curtain circles.

He is a fourth-generation San Franciscan and the grandson of a Barbary Coast dancehall girl.

Gossage was the Socrates of San Francisco. The visiting lions from Tom Wolfe to Terry Thomas came to call on him in the magnificently restored old firehouse on Pacific Street that was his place of work and, for a time, when Howard and his buddy Herb Caen were both between marriages and batching it about town, place of residence. Gossage operated the Firehouse as if it were a French court, and he the captive King. He did everything first class — he ate, flew, wrote, talked, traveled first class. He believed every man should be comfortable while engaging in the necessary business of rescuing the world. He was at the same time as open and innocent as a doe-eyed calf and as crafty as a raunchy old owl.

Warren Hinckle,
IF YOU HAVE A LEMON, MAKE
LEMONADE

Eric Hoffer

At an early age, Eric Hoffer (1902–   ) figured out several important things: "One, that I didn't want to work in a factory; two, that I couldn't stand being dependent on the good graces of a boss; three, that I was going to stay poor; four, that I had to get out of New York. Logic told me that California was the poor man's country."

So Hoffer came to California. In old-fashioned, almost-forgotten ways he exemplifies the Western spirit of individualism the state has traditionally nurtured so well. He is a self-educated scholar who prefers blue-collar labor to the more genteel and certainly more financially rewarding life he could have if he accepted the many lecturing invitations he receives.

Hoffer had a miserable childhood made worse by an accident that blinded him for eight years. At age eighteen, with no formal education, no experience at making a living, and both parents dead, he headed for Los Angeles with a basketful of books.

For three years he worked in a box factory; when he had saved $200, he took two months off to read. Next, he worked as a migrant farm laborer, then as a railroad hand, lumberjack, and dishwasher. He had library cards in a dozen towns.

He began writing in the 1930s and in 1941 sent some articles to Margaret Anderson, editor of the magazine *Common Ground.* Anderson sent them to Harper & Brothers, which later became his first publisher.

In 1943 he became a longshoreman on San Francisco's waterfront, a job that afforded him "freedom, exercise, leisure and income," since he needed to work only two or three days a week to support his writing habit.

When his most famous book, *The True Believer,* was published in 1951, a *New Yorker* critic described Hoffer as "a born generalizer with a mind that inclines to the wry epigram and the aphorism as naturally as did that of the Duc de la Rochefoucauld."

What kind of people were the early settlers and miners? I asked. They were a hard-working, tough lot, I was told. They drank, fought, gambled and wenched. They wallowed in luxury or lived on next to nothing with equal ease. They were the salt of the earth.

Still it is not clear what manner of people they were.

If I asked what they looked like, I was told of whiskers, broad-brimmed hats, high boots, shirts of many colors, suntanned faces, horny hands. Finally I asked: What group of people in present-day California most closely resembles the pioneers? The answer, usually after some hesitation, was invariably the same: "the Okies and fruit tramps."

Eric Hoffer,
THE ORDEAL OF CHANGE

Helen Holdredge

Helen Holdredge had already written several novels before the work she considers her true writing career began in 1930.

By that time, she had left her native Duluth, attended St. Mary's Academy in Portland, and married Claire Holdredge, an explorer and geologist. The Holdredges would eventually live in thirty-four American cities and South America, but the marriage was only four years old when they discovered the diaries of Teresa Bell, a protégée of the mysterious Mammy Pleasant.

Bell had given the diaries to Helen's father, who had stored them in a cupboard over a fireplace at a house the family owned in Vancouver, Washington. The Holdredges found them when they were restoring the house.

Instantly fascinated by the diaries, Helen began work on a biography of Mammy Pleasant, researching it by interviewing the sons and daughters of former slaves. As a biographer, she had to learn her craft as a writer all over again: "I had to learn never to do anything unless I had a fact to back it up." Yet she loved the work so much that she speaks of her novels as "a closed subject. I don't want to revive that period."

After *Mammy Pleasant*, Holdredge wrote *Mammy Pleasant's Partner*, *The Woman in Black* (about Lola Montez), *The House of the Strange Woman* (about Isaiah Lees, an early San Francisco police chief), and *Firebelle Lillie* (about Lillie Coit).

"All my books are about San Francisco and its history," she says. "I just got started with Teresa Bell's diary, and I went on from there. I built up a monumental pile of research, and I'm still drawing on it."

Holdredge, who lives in Torrance, California, declines to reveal her age.

ary Ellen liked to brag that she "held the key to every closet in town with a skeleton in it." She knew just which dowager in San Francisco had arrived masquerading as the wife of the man she accompanied; which woman had had an illegitimate baby before her marriage. She knew, too, the men living under assumed names, was aware of the records of those who were remittance men, those who had committed murders and those who had deserted their families elsewhere. As early as 1857 these people had made a practice of sending her an invitation to their parties, to which she always sent her "regrets."

Helen Holdredge,
MAMMY PLEASANT

Jack Kerouac

Though Jack Kerouac (1922–1969) never lived for very long in San Francisco, he made it a place of mystery and delight for the thousands of Eastern and Midwestern college students who gobbled up his work in the late 1950s and early 1960s.

"San Francisco, the white sky bright cry paradise . . . Jack's Oriental mysterious seaport city . . .," wrote Barry Gifford in the *Yale Literary Magazine.* "No one wrote of it more regally."

Kerouac's hometown was Lowell, Massachusetts. After a brief sojourn at Columbia University, he chucked a football scholarship to become a merchant mariner.

He held the occasional job after that, but mostly he travelled the country at breakneck speed, clutching to his bosom adventure and novelty. He was able to sit still long enough to write and painstakingly rewrite his first novel, *The Town and the City,* over a three-year period. He never did it again. He wrote *On the Road,* his best-known and most popular book, in three weeks, typing on rolls of glued-together art paper.

Kerouac called his form the "bookmovie" and defended it thus: "My work comprises one vast book like Proust's *Remembrance of Things Past,* except that my remembrances are written on the run instead of afterward in a sickbed." Not all critics were impressed; some applied to him the worst of all literary epithets — boring. But he came to be *the* novelist of the beat generation, as Allen Ginsberg was its poet.

Once, referring to a friend named Herbert Huncke, he was so foolish as to try to define the word "beat." "To me," he said, "it meant being poor, like sleeping in the subways, like Huncke used to do, and yet being illuminated and having illuminated ideas about apocalypse and all that. . . ."

Later he decided "beat" meant "beatific."

Meanwhile scores of people stood around in the darkened gallery straining to hear every word of the poetry reading as I wandered from group to group, facing them and facing away from the stage, urging them to glug a slug from the jug, or wandered back and sat on the right side of the stage giving out little wows and yesses of approval and even whole sentences of comment with nobody's invitation but in the general gaiety nobody's disapproval either. It was a great night. Delicate Francis Da Pavia read, from delicate onionskin yellow pages, or pink which he kept flipping carefully with long white fingers, the poems of his dead chum Altman who'd eaten too much peyote in Chihuahua (or died of polio, one) but read none of his own poems — a charming elegy in itself to the memory of the dead young poet, enough to draw tears from the Cervantes of Chapter Seven, and read them in a delicate Englishy voice that had me crying with inside laughter though I later got to know Francis and liked him.

Jack Kerouac,
THE DHARMA BUMS

Theodora Kroeber

"Some people are through at forty. And others are just getting started," Theodora Kroeber (1897–1979) once remarked.

Kroeber herself was an inspiration to late-blooming writers and aging women. She wrote her first book at age fifty-five, and at seventy-one she married her third husband, a young man of twenty-seven.

She came from Colorado to Berkeley to study at the University of California and, after a brief first marriage that left her a widow, married one of her professors, anthropologist Alfred L. Kroeber.

She and Kroeber had four children, one of whom is the writer Ursula LeGuin. Though she was later to be called an anthropologist and a historian, her undergraduate and graduate degrees were in psychology.

Ishi in Two Worlds, her most famous book, was published in 1961, the year of Alfred Kroeber's death. The story of the last living Yahi Indian, who lived out his final years at the university museum, was far more successful than anyone dreamed it would be and made Theodora a great deal more famous than Alfred.

After her husband died, she continued to write and to live in the Berkeley house she had shared with him for decades. In 1966 she married John Quinn, a psychologist and painter.

In 1977, during her eightieth year, Governor Edmund G. Brown, Jr., appointed her to the University of California Board of Regents on the grounds that he was "troubled by the mundane level of discussion at the regents' meetings" and needed someone to talk to.

She died at home at age eighty-two.

Golden Gate Park was only three blocks from the museum. Pope and Ishi went to the park for their archery practice. Occasionally Ishi went there alone: he followed the park's meandering paths and came close to animals and birds with his noiseless tread, or he sat still, watching the captive herd of buffalo, learning the look and ways of these strange and surprising creatures.

The street on which he shopped, the streetcar which passed the museum entrance, Golden Gate Park which lay in full view from the museum, became Ishi's new world. Looking down over city and park, he could follow with his eyes the circle of his world's boundaries — the limit of its extent and its invisible borders. Kroeber says that Ishi could no doubt have mapped it accurately, as he mapped his old Yana world.

Theodora Kroeber,
ISHI IN TWO WORLDS

C.Y. Lee

In *The Flower Drum Song,* C. Y. Lee (1917–) wrote with gentle affection about San Francisco's Chinatown and, so far as most of the world is concerned, put Grant Avenue on the map when the book became the basis of a Rodgers and Hammerstein musical.

"When people ask me where I am from, I always say San Francisco," Lee once wrote. "Some will stare and others will raise an eyebrow inquisitively. 'Are you one of the rare native sons?'

"'Yes,' I'll answer, 'I'm one of the adopted native sons.' Then the invariable question: 'Why do you like San Francisco?' To me this a hard question to answer . . .

"What makes a man want to live here? Sure, you can say here is the city where you can live like a hermit or busybody, you can eat all types of food, you can become a beatnik or lead an intellectual life of the highest order. You have a lot of mobility and freedom (except for parking space); you have tolerance and plenty of intellectual and spiritual elbow room. You have everything a big city can supply and yet in fifteen minutes you can be in the jungles of the Sausalito hills, overlooking the beautiful bay and the ocean. But it isn't all this that attracts me. I think it's the friendliness, the warmth and honesty of the majority of the people in the Bay Area that make a fellow want to settle down here."

Lee was raised in Hunan province in China, escaping to Yunan during the Japanese invasion. In 1943 he came to the United States to study at Columbia and Yale. Eight years later he settled in San Francisco, where he worked for a Chinatown newspaper and wrote novels.

Because he felt safe now, he sometimes sauntered out of Grant Avenue and ventured to some side streets and back alleys. He discovered, to his surprise, many sights and noises that were both strange and familiar to him. The clatter of mahjongg behind the closed doors, the operatic music of drums and gongs from basements with signs saying "Music Club," the noodle factories, and tailor shops with children playing around their working mothers, the pawnshops with the high counter, the barbershops with all the traditional services, including cleaning the ears and beating the shoulders, the retired old men reading the Chinese newspapers in little stores which sell nothing . . . all these were familiar to him, reminding him of China.

C. Y. Lee,
THE FLOWER DRUM SONG

Ella Leffland

One morning Ella Leffland (1931–   ) woke up and thought, "My whole life is going to bed, getting up, and writing. It's like a prison." Then she got up, had her first cup of coffee, wrote her first sentence of the day, and "all the pleasure flowed back."

She started writing as a seven-year-old child in Martinez, California. At fourteen, she began submitting her stories to magazines — hand-printed, since she didn't have a typewriter.

The day before her twenty-eighth birthday, "Eino," her first published story, appeared in *The New Yorker,* but it was another four years before the second appeared in print.

Leffland is a careful craftswoman who frequently gets up at 5:30 A.M. and keeps writing until eight or nine P.M., turning out "a salvageable page and a half a day." Her stories have now been collected in *Best Short Stories of 1970* and *O. Henry Best Short Stories of 1976,* and she has published three novels.

In *Mrs. Munck* and *Rumors of Peace,* she used the Carquinez Straits area of her youth as her setting, and in *Love Out of Season,* she used San Francisco.

"I feel very bound to this area — Port Costa and Martinez," she said. "I wanted to show its kind of authentic isolation. It's very untouched by progress and has a very old-fashioned, individual kind of feeling.

"I feel San Francisco is that way too. It seems to have retained a great deal of individuality, and it was the starting point of many avant-garde movements such as the flower children, which is what *Love Out of Season* is about."

One Saturday afternoon she went with some girls
from the Y to the Haight — a wilderness of
costumed youths and girls, leaping dogs, yawning
babies carried on backs, guitars, bongos, beaded
doorways, drifts of incense and some other sweet smell,
and throughout it all, like a warm wind, smiles of
welcome. None of this had been there a few months ago; it
had sprung up overnight, a dazzling carnival. She found
strangers saying hello to her; someone gave her a yellow
daisy, someone else a string of wooden beads. She began
stooping to pet the heads of the smaller dogs, but she
didn't have the courage to respond to anyone else, and
when she lost her friends in the crowd she grew uneasy and
took the bus home.

Ella Leffland,
LOVE OUT OF SEASON

Oscar Lewis

A list of books by Oscar Lewis (1893–   ) reads like the table of contents for a local history textbook. "For sixty-five years," wrote Kevin Starr in 1977, "he has sought to do one thing — write well about the city of San Francisco and the state of California."

A sampling of book titles: *San Francisco: Mission to Metropolis, Bay Window Bohemia: An Account of the Brilliant Artistic World of Gaslit San Francisco, Sutter's Fort: Gateway to the Gold Fields,* and *This Was San Francisco.*

Then there are booklets: *The Origin of the Celebrated Jumping Frog of Calaveras County, The California Mining Towns,* and *Fabulous San Simeon.*

Though Lewis is certainly a historian, he isn't a scholar in the usual sense. Following the advice of one of his professors at the University of California, Berkeley, Lewis quit school, installed himself and his typewriter in a rented office, and got to be a writer by writing.

A San Francisco native, he grew up in Sebastopol, Red Bluff, and Berkeley, as well as the city. When he started writing, he specialized in stories for boys, selling his work steadily to young people's magazines from 1914 to 1920. Then he moved on to the general magazine field and in 1930 began his true vocation as a West Coast historian.

From 1948 to 1960 he was a member of the San Francisco Art Commission. He still lives in his home town, a few blocks from the house where he was born at Jackson and Baker streets.

Huntington's dislike for California and, in particular, for San Francisco increased as he grew older. He had a theory that mild climate bred weaklings; a man who didn't have to fight the weather was unlikely to fight anything else. There were other reasons, less theoretical. Stanford's continued prestige on the Coast was persistently irritating, and the expense of preventing the passage or enforcement of anti-railroad legislation at Sacramento seemed to him far too high. There were also the sustained and bitter attacks on him by San Francisco newspapers, led by the *Examiner,* on the editorial page of which a then unknown cartoonist, one Homer Davenport, daily pictured him with his hands in the pockets of the common people, a design of dollar signs ornamenting his enormous paunch.

Oscar Lewis,
THE BIG FOUR

Jack London

Jack London (1876–1916) is arguably the greatest writer produced by the Bay Area — and certainly one of the most colorful. Some might say that London's pose as an adventurer and Great Lover came from a sense of insecurity over his short stature — he was five-feet-eight — or over the facts of his birth — he was the illegitimate son of a Wisconsin-born woman and an itinerant Irish astrologer. They might also say he became a Socialist because his childhood was wretchedly poor. But they might never explain how such a man became a writer so painstaking that he worked fifteen hours a day.

Although his childhood years in Oakland were spent mostly in the public library, his teen years included terms as an oyster pirate, longshoreman, seaman, and tramp. At nineteen, he went back to Oakland High School and even to the University of California for a semester or so, but left school to get a job in a laundry.

In 1896 he caught gold fever and went to the Klondike. He returned with no gold but with experiences he would later draw on to write his most popular novel, *Call of the Wild.*

Though he began to write while he was longshoring in his mid-teens, he failed to sell anything until 1899, when the *Overland Monthly* bought one of his short stories. Then *Black Cat* and the *Atlantic Monthly* bought more stories, and a New York publisher bought a collection of them, which was to become London's first book, *The Son of the Wolf.*

During the next sixteen years, London turned out some fifty volumes, all the while living a life that kept him in the public eye. His honeymoon cruise of the South Sea Islands with his second wife, Charmian, was well covered by the press, as was his every petty argument.

London died at age forty, officially of uremic poisoning, though two empty morphine vials were found by his bed, along with a pad on which the lethal dosage of the drug had been calculated.

We must have been struck squarely amidships, for I saw nothing, the strange steamboat having passed beyond my line of vision. The *Martinez* heeled over sharply, and there was a crashing and rending of timber. I was thrown flat on the wet deck and before I could scramble to my feet I heard the scream of the women. This it was, I am certain — the most indescribable of blood-curdling sounds — that threw me into a panic. I remembered the life-preservers stored in the cabin, but was met at the door and swept backward by a wild rush of men and women. What happened in the next few minutes I do not recollect, though I have a clear remembrance of pulling down life-preservers from the overhead racks, while the red-faced man fastened them about the bodies of an hysterical group of women. This memory is as distinct and sharp as that of any picture I have seen. It is a picture, and I can see it now — the jagged edges of the hole in the side of the cabin, through which gray fog swirled and eddied; empty upholstered seats, littered with all the evidences of sudden flight, such as packages, hand satchels, umbrellas and wraps; the stout gentleman who had been reading my essay, encased in cork and canvas, the magazine still in his hand and asking me with monotonous insistence if I thought there was any danger; the red-faced man, stumping gallantly around on his artificial legs and buckling life-preservers on all comers; and finally, the screaming bedlam of women.

Jack London,
THE SEA WOLF

Frank Norris

Frank Norris (1870–1902), considered one of America's great pioneer realists, moved to San Francisco with his Chicago family in his early teens. They lived in the Polk Street district, then a semi-slum area of small stores that was to become the setting for *McTeague,* Norris's masterpiece.

Deciding that young Frank had a gift for drawing, his family sent him to art school in Paris, but he frittered away his time writing medieval romances. When his father discovered what Frank was up to, he ordered him home at once.

Next, Frank was sent to the University of California to study mathematics. He flunked out, but not before he discovered Emile Zola and determined to be the first American realist.

His writing career began in journalism. He covered the Boer War for the *San Francisco Chronicle,* then joined the staff of the *Wave,* a magazine that was attracting most of the local literati.

In 1898, he left for New York to join the staff of *McClure's* magazine and he published his first novel, *Moran of the Lady Letty.* After a trip to Cuba to cover the Spanish-American war for *McClure's,* Norris became a reader for Doubleday, Page & Co.

McTeague, the careful study of devastation wrought on the family of a Polk Street advertising dentist by miserliness, was published in 1899.

Norris married in 1900, moved back to California, and devoted himself to a projected trilogy on the growth, sale, and consumption of wheat. The first volume, *The Octopus,* which relates the struggle for power between the California wheat ranchers and the railroad, is considered far superior to its sequel, *The Pit,* which tells of an attempt to corner the wheat market in the stock exchange.

Norris never wrote the third book. He died at thirty-two of appendicitis.

And so she went out, this last Argo, loaded with gold seekers from a land of gold, went out with the outgoing tide; and after the excitement was over and the ship gone from sight, we others, you and I and all the rest of us, set our faces cityward and thought to ourselves, "Well she's gone, and we ain't in her, and if that fool Batty comes back with a wad, I'll kick myself around the whole dam' lot for not goin'."

Frank Norris, "Sailing of the Excelsior"
from COLLECTED WRITINGS

Kathleen Norris

In 1935 Kathleen Norris (1880–1966) was making more than $300,000 a year and was said to be the highest paid woman in America. Her first novel, *Mother,* sold 750,000 copies in its first year, and she wrote nearly eighty others.

Born into a socially prominent San Francisco family, she was reared in the pre-earthquake city of romance and gaslights. At nineteen, she was about to make her debut when both her parents died, leaving the family nearly penniless. She took any work she could get to support her five younger brothers and sisters, finally becoming a society reporter for the *San Francisco Examiner.*

During those years, wrote historian Kevin Starr, "she gathered in details of the cityscape which enlivened her fiction; the details of everyday San Francisco life — boarding houses, offices, department stores, shops, restaurants, places to go on Sunday — so marvelously present, say, in *Saturday's Child,* the finest novel she ever wrote."

In 1909, she married Charles "Cigi" Norris, the brother of author Frank Norris. They moved to New York, where Cigi had a job as art editor of *American Magazine,* and set up housekeeping on $50 — two weeks' pay.

Almost immediately, Kathleen sold a short story to the *Atlantic Monthly* and six more to *McClure's* magazine. A short version of *Mother* appeared first in the *American.*

Mother and most of Norris's other books are based on her belief in happiness through the domestic life.

In time, Norris's husband also became a novelist, and the pair moved back to California in 1919 — this time to a ranch at Saratoga, where they became legendary entertainers, sponsoring amateur theatricals and croquet games for the likes of Theodore Roosevelt, Jr., Charles Lindbergh, Edna Ferber, and George S. Kaufman.

Girls married drinkers, to "reform them," and succeeded or failed with equal equanimity. Girls married rakes, and patiently followed their fortunes into long struggles for subsistence, for children's needs, or dim hopes of regained solvency and restored self-respect. Girls married the bubble-made pioneer millionaires and went from humble homes to the magnificence of Nob Hill, driving behind their matched grays, among the sand hills and the young green of Golden Gate Park, wearing their diamonds at entertainments that rivalled the Arabian Nights in extravagant splendor.

But no engaged girl ever thought seriously of the future. They might all have been convinced that the story ended with the familiar promise of living happily ever after. The marriage was the exciting — the desirable, goal. After that, well, at least one was married.

Kathleen Norris,
MISS HARRIET TOWNSHEND

Tillie Olsen

As a young woman of nineteen, Tillie Olsen (1913–   ) began a book called *Yonnondio: From the Thirties,* and the first chapter was published in the newly established *Partisan Review.* A critic called it "a work of early genius," but Olsen didn't know about it — she was in jail at the time.

It was 1934, and Olsen was an active union member; she was arrested as a result of the general strike that year. Throughout the next few years she was deeply involved with what she calls "the great movements of the '30s" and with the problems of raising her first child. She did not write again for twenty years.

She collected data, though, working in warehouses, as a waitress, as a hotel maid, as an office typist, and raising four daughters who went to San Francisco public schools. "I must have worked in at least a hundred different San Francisco places," she says. "I have a family and work knowledge of San Francisco that few writers have."

Tell Me a Riddle, a collection of stories, was published in 1961, when Olsen was nearly fifty, followed by *Yonnondio* in 1974 and *Silences* in 1978.

Some of the stories in *Tell Me a Riddle* have been anthologized nearly forty times, and Olsen has been heaped with every kind of honor a writer can receive — grants, teaching posts, prizes, and critical acclaim.

Although she is from Omaha, she says quite firmly that, "I am a San Franciscan. It is ineradicable in me."

The junior high school in her story "Oh, Yes" is based on one her daughter went to; the black church in the same story is a composite of three churches she knows in the Fillmore District. But Olsen's sense of place is as vivid in her characters as in her settings.

"Working and raising children in San Francisco," she says, "gave me access to human beings of all colors in a way that's a rare privilege for a writer. It is a city where you do not have to live a ghettoized life."

And so he gets there after all, four days and everything else too late. It is an old peaked house on a hill and he has imaged and entered it over and over again, in a thousand various places a thousand various times: on watch and over chow, lying on his bunk or breezing with the guys; from sidewalk beds and doorway shelters, in flophouses and jails; sitting silent at union meetings or waiting in the places one waits, or listening to the Come to Jesus boys.

Tillie Olsen, "Hey Sailor, What Ship?"
from TELL ME A RIDDLE

Josiah Royce

Though Josiah Royce (1855–1916) is best known for his famous theory of the Absolute, he also cast a philosopher's eye on his native state, perhaps with special personal interest. His own parents suffered risk and hardship to go there during the gold rush.

Born in Grass Valley, California, Royce was educated at home until he was eleven. When the family moved to San Francisco, he enrolled in school and installed himself in the Mercantile Library, where he read voraciously.

At the University of California he was inspired to go on to further study of philosophy in Germany and at Johns Hopkins University.

For several years after receiving his Ph.D., he taught English literature at the University of California and became an assistant professor at Harvard in 1885. He continued to climb the academic ladder at that university until, in 1914, he became Alford Professor of Natural Religion, Moral Philosophy, and Civil Polity.

The year Royce went to Harvard, *The Religious Aspect of Philosophy,* the book that established his theory of the Absolute, was published. Royce held that if one admits the possibility of evil, then an absolute principle of Truth, an all-knowing Mind or Universal Thought, must follow.

The theory gave other philosophers of his day, including William James and George Santayana, many pleasurable hours of debate and made Royce for twenty-five years the leading American exponent of post-Kantian idealism.

California: A Study of American Character was published in 1886. It was followed by numerous other books, including one novel, *The Feud of Oakfield Creek,* which received an unenthusiastic public welcome.

Society in these years was affected first of all by certain obvious and general mental disturbances of individual lives — disturbances that had a decidedly pathological character. Most of the citizens were young men, and homeless. Their daily and most sober business was at best dangerously near gambling, and their nerves were constantly tormented by unnatural and yet for the time inevitable excitements of a perilously violent sort. They differed, moreover, from the miners in that their life was as a rule comparatively sedentary and in that they worked far more with their brains than with their hands. Hence these nervous excitements told upon them all the more seriously.

Josiah Royce,
CALIFORNIA: A STUDY
OF AMERICAN CHARACTER

William Saroyan

In the mid-1930s, a time of unhappiness and cynicism, William Saroyan (1908–   ) bustled onto the literary scene, all exuberance and sentiment, and critics called him "the most significant talent to appear in San Francisco since Frank Norris and Jack London."

Saroyan couldn't have put it better himself. "I am so innately great," he once noted," "that by comparison others who believe they are great or act as if they are great seem to me to be only pathetic, though occasionally charming."

Born into a poor Armenian family in Fresno, California, Saroyan "discovered" that he was a writer at thirteen and promptly transferred to a technical high school to learn typing. Confident he had as much education as he needed, he dropped out of school at fifteen and became a telegraph messenger. He moved from that career into so many others so fast that the employment agencies quit recommending him.

At seventeen, he went to San Francisco and settled down to do his writing apprenticeship while working as a manager of a telegraph office. In 1933 he sold a story to an Armenian magazine; the next year he sold another — "Daring Young Man on the Flying Trapeze — to *Story* magazine.

In 1939 he became a playwright, with *My Heart's in the Highlands,* and in 1940, *The Time of Your Life* won both the New York Drama Critics' Circle Award and the Pulitzer Prize. Saroyan declined to accept the latter on grounds that wealth should not patronize art.

Saroyan has since published hundreds of stories, essays, novels, plays, and autobiographical sketches, but many of his plays have not done well, and he has received scant critical praise for his novels. The short story is his real medium. "Probably since O. Henry," wrote one critic, "nobody has done more than William Saroyan to endear and stabilize [that form]."

Nick (*watching*): I run the lousiest dive in Frisco, and a guy arrives and makes me stock up with champagne. The whores come and holler at me that they're ladies. Talent comes in and begs me for a chance to show itself. Even society people come in once in a while. I don't know what for. Maybe it's liquor. Maybe it's the location. Maybe it's my personality. Maybe it's the crazy personality of the joint. The old honkytonk. (*pause*) Maybe they can't feel at home anywhere else.

William Saroyan,
THE TIME OF YOUR LIFE

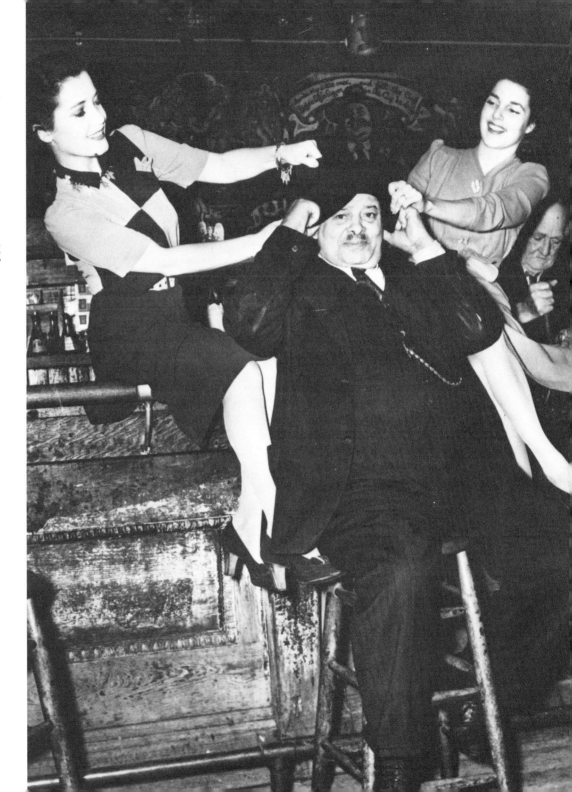

George Sterling

George Sterling (1869–1926) called San Francisco "the Cool Gray City of Love" and its citizens called him a number of things, including the "Uncrowned King of Bohemia" and their poet laureate.

His poetry was practically unknown in the East, while in the West he was compared to Shakespeare, Euripides, Shelley, and Poe. Despite such weaknesses as alcohol and women, he was as lovable as he was colorful.

A native of Long Island, New York, he never finished college and had seemingly no bent for any profession. So his family sent him to San Francisco to work for his uncle, a wealthy realtor. For fifteen years, very much against his will, he toiled in his uncle's office until his aunt gave him "freedom money" to devote his time to writing.

His two great influences were Ambrose Bierce, whose rigid literary dogmas were said to have had "lamentable" effects on Sterling's style, and Jack London, who introduced him to the bohemian life. Sterling's gusto for that lifestyle made him a constant source of entertainment. He held court at Joseph Coppa's restaurant in the Montgomery Block and was once arrested for wading in Stow Lake at midnight with an undraped young woman. He paid his fine with autographed books.

His wife, complaining of "poet's temperament," divorced him in 1912 and committed suicide the next year. Another of his loves, Nora May French, also took cyanide and walked into the sea at Carmel.

During his last years, Sterling lived at the Bohemian Club. Shortly before his fifty-seventh birthday, he too took cyanide. Newspaper accounts of the day said he was depressed about ill health, and some historians say he was upset because his powers as a writer were failing. Others say, however, that he swallowed the poison in a fit of pique at being replaced as toastmaster for a dinner honoring H. L. Mencken.

He was so much a part of the San Francisco landscape that his colleague Idwal Jones remarked that "it was like a unicorn dying."

Within the House of Mammon there is no need of song,
And faced by them who doubt not, no doubt endures for long;
Tho twilight hold the temple, there yet each one shall see
The Word of Words, the letters that spell "Necessity."

George Sterling,
from "The Common Cult"

Robert Louis Stevenson

Although Robert Louis Stevenson (1850–1894) stayed only briefly in San Francisco, his sojourn was nothing if not romantic — he was there to join the woman he loved.

She was an American, Fanny Vandegrift Osbourne, whom he had met in Fontainebleau while she was separated from her husband. The couple's involvement lasted, much to the horror of Stevenson's parents, who had already suffered a number of bitter disappointments at their son's hands. Fanny was not only married but ten years Robert's senior, and the elder Stevensons were vastly relieved when she returned to California. Robert followed, however, ill and penniless after an arduous trip he later wrote about in *The Amateur Emigrant* and *Across the Plains*. Stevenson made a living in any way he could, dividing his time between San Francisco and Monterey. Eventually, Fanny was divorced, and she and Stevenson married. They had a honeymoon by an abandoned silver mine — recorded in *The Silverado Squatters* — and then sailed for Scotland to reconcile with Robert's parents.

Early in life Stevenson figured out that he was not happy in stodgy Edinburgh where he had grown up and that he had no vocation to be a lighthouse engineer, as his family wished. He agreed to study law, however, and adopted a bohemian viewpoint while at university.

He never practiced law but traveled instead, writing essays as he went. He and Fanny continued to move frequently, always seeking a healthy climate since Stevenson was severely tubercular. He wrote wherever they settled, with three years in Bournemouth proving particularly productive. He wrote *Kidnapped* and *The Strange Case of Dr. Jekyll and Mr. Hyde* there.

The Stevensons returned to San Francisco briefly in 1888 on their way to the South Seas, where they remained for the rest of Stevenson's life. They settled finally in Samoa, where Stevenson's respiratory ailment left him alone. A cerebral hemorrhage killed him at age forty-four.

The day was breaking as we crossed the ferry; the fog was rising over the citied hills of San Francisco; the bay was perfect — not a ripple, scarce a stain, upon its blue expanse; everything was waiting, breathless, for the sun. A spot of cloudy gold lit first upon the head of Tamalpais, and then widened downward on its shapely shoulder; the air seemed to awaken, and began to sparkle; and suddenly

"The tall hills Titan discovered,"

and the city of San Francisco, and the bay of gold and corn, were lit from end to end with summer daylight.

Robert Louis Stevenson,
ACROSS THE PLAINS

George R. Stewart

George R. Stewart (1895–   ), a native of Sewickley, Pennsylvania, first made his way to California as a graduate student in the English department at Berkeley. After taking his Ph.D. at Columbia, then working briefly at the University of Michigan, he came back as an instructor.

For awhile he wrote scholarly articles, then a book called *The Techniques of English Verse* and a life of Bret Harte. During the depression years university advancement was slow and discouraging, so Stewart turned to nonacademic writing in 1936 with *Ordeal by Hunger* a critically and popularly successful account of the Donner party. In that book and the ones that followed, Stewart displayed the passion for precision and detail he had learned as an academic.

The way he researched *Storm,* his best-known book, in which he describes the genesis, growth, and devastation wrought by a wind named Maria, is legendary. He watched storms in the San Francisco Bay, taking notes as they lashed the city. He pestered the life out of the Weather Bureau. He hitched rides on snowplows in the mountains. The book, in which the weather is actually a character, was hailed as a new novel form. It was followed in 1948 by *Fire.* The two books have frequently been assigned as reading in college meteorology and forestry courses.

Stewart's own best-loved book is *Names on the Land,* which he considers his most important contribution to scholarship. In a *San Francisco Examiner* story about Stewart, Mickey Friedman called the book "a hilarious account of the year-and-a-half struggle to find a name for Berkeley" and "a wonderful spoof of committee endeavor."

Stewart gave Friedman a marvelous illustration of the depth of his attention to detail. "I do a great deal of work on my prose style," he said. "I don't think you'll find the past tense of 'did' — 'did not' or 'didn't' — in *Names on the Land* at all. I thought it was ugly."

On the surface, to the eye, they had changed. The towers that hid their tips in the summer clouds, the mile-long dipping cable, the interlocked massive beams of steel — no longer they cast back the morning sun with a bright sheen of silver gray. Over them now rested softly the neutral pall of rust, red-brown color of desolation. Only at the tops of the towers, and along the cables at good spots for perching, the quiet monotone was capped and spotted with the dead-white smears of the droppings of birds.

Yes, through the years the sea-birds had perched there — the gulls and pelicans and cormorants. And on the piers the rats scurried and fought, and bred and nested, and lived as only rats can — squeaking and fighting, and breeding and nesting, and at low tide feeding on mussels and crabs.

The broad roadway, unused, showed a few signs of change — only roughnesses and a few cracks here and there. Where blown dust had settled into cracks and corners, a little grass was growing, and a few hardy weeds, not many.

George R. Stewart,
EARTH ABIDES

Mark Twain

By the time Mark Twain (also Samuel Langhorne Clemens, 1835–1910) came to San Francisco, he had already distinguished himself as a practitioner of a certain playful kind of journalism.

He arrived in 1864, secured a job on the *Morning Call,* and joined the vigorous bohemia that nurtured Bret Harte, Charles Warren Stoddard, and others writing for the *Golden Era,* the *Alta California,* and later the *Overland Monthly.* Twain's first attempts at humor are invariably described as "crude," but, under the tutelage of Bret Harte, he got the knack of story-telling. His writing acquired sophistication and a satirical strain.

Harte is said to have helped him craft his story "The Celebrated Jumping Frog of Calaveras County," which was published in 1865 by the *New York Saturday Press.* It was an immediate smash hit, and Twain was a nationally famous humorist overnight.

Twain found San Francisco dull after his previous careers as a pilot on the Mississippi and a reporter in exuberant Virginia City, Nevada. So it was a lucky thing the *Sacramento Union* decided to send him on a tour of Hawaii (then the Sandwich Islands), and then the world.

Innocents Abroad, his first book (aside from a collection of short stories), came out of the world tour. It was published in 1869, and a steady stream of others followed. "It is my habit," Twain once wrote in a letter, "to keep four or five books in process of erection all the time and every summer add a few courses of bricks to two or three of them . . . It takes seven years to complete a book by this method but still it is a good method: give the public a rest."

In 1869, Twain bought a part interest in the *Buffalo Express,* which he edited for two years. In 1871 he moved to Connecticut, where he lived for the rest of his life. He was born under Halley's Comet and always said he'd die the next time the comet came around. He did.

From the moment we left the stable, the fog was so thick that we could scarcely see fifty yards behind or before, or overhead and for a while, as we approached the Cliff House, we could not see the horse at all, and were obliged to steer by his ears, which stood up dimly out of the dense white mist that enveloped him. But for these friendly beacons, we might have been cast away and lost.

I have no opinion of a six-mile ride in the clouds; but if I ever have to take another, I want to leave the horse in the stable and go in a balloon. I shall prefer to go in the afternoon, also, when it is warm, so that I may gape, and yawn, and stretch if I am drowsy, without disarranging my horse-blanket and letting in a blast of cold wind.

We could scarcely see the sportive seals out on the rocks, writhing and squirming like exaggerated maggots, and there was nothing soothing in their discordant barking, to a spirit so depressed as mine was.

Mark Twain,
in the GOLDEN ERA

Bibliography

ALICE ADAMS
Beautiful Girl. Knopf, 1978.
Careless Love. New American Library, 1966.
The Fall of Daisy Duke. Constable, 1967. (English edition of *Careless Love.*)
Families and Survivors. Knopf, 1974.
Listening to Billie. Knopf, 1978.

MAYA ANGELOU
And Still I Rise. Random, 1978.
Gather Together in My Name. Random, 1974.
I Know Why the Caged Bird Sings. Random, 1970.
Just Give Me a Cool Drink of Water 'Fore I Diiie. Random, 1971.
Oh Pray My Wings Are Gonna Fit Me Well. Random, 1975.
Singin' and Swingin' and Gettin' Merry Like Christmas. Random, 1976.

DON ASHER
Blood Summer. Putnam, 1977.
Don't the Moon Look Lonesome. Atheneum, 1967.
The Electric Cotillion. Doubleday, 1970.
The Eminent Yachtsman and the Whorehouse Piano Player. Coward, McCann, & Geoghegan, 1973.
Honeycomb: Ballad of a North Beach Cabaret. California Living Books, 1979.
The Piano Sport. Atheneum, 1966.
Raise Up Off Me. Coward, McCann, & Geoghegan, 1974. (Co-author, Hampton Hawes.)

GERTRUDE ATHERTON
Adventures of a Novelist. Liveright, 1932. (Autobiography.)
American Wives and English Husbands. Dodd, Mead, 1898. (Republished in 1919 as *Transplanted.*)
Ancestors; a novel. Harper, 1907.
The Aristocrats; being the impressions of the Lady Helen Pole during her sojourn in the great woods as spontaneously recorded in her letters to her friend in North Britain, the Countess of Edge and Ross. B. W. Dodge, 1901.
The Avalanche; a mystery story. Frederick A. Stokes, 1919.
Before the Gringo Came. Selwin Tait, 1894. (Reissued in 1902 as *The Splendid Idle Forties.*)
The Bell in the Fog, and Other Stories. Harper, 1905.
Black Oxen. Boni & Liveright, 1923.
California: An Intimate History. Harper, 1914; Boni & Liveright, 1927 (revised and enlarged).
The Californians. Lane, 1898.
Can Women Be Gentlemen? Houghton Mifflin, 1938.
Los Cerritos; a romance of the modern time. John Lovell, 1890.
The Conqueror; being the true and romantic story of Alexander Hamilton. Macmillan, 1902.
The Crystal Cup. Boni & Liveright, 1925.
A Daughter of the Vine. Lane, 1899. (Same as *Rudolph of Redwood.*)
Dido, Queen of Hearts. Liveright, 1929.
The Doomswoman; an historical romance of Old California. Tait, 1893.
Foghorn; stories. Houghton Mifflin, 1934.
Golden Gate Country. Duell, Sloan, and Pearce, 1945.
Golden Peacock. Houghton Mifflin, 1936.
The Gorgeous Isle; a romance; scene: Nevis, B. W. I., 1842. Doubleday, 1908.
Hermia Suydam. Current Literature Publishing, 1889.
His Fortunate Grace. Appleton, 1897.
The Horn of Life. Appleton-Century, 1942.
The House of Lee. Appleton-Century, 1940.
The Immortal Marriage. Boni & Liveright, 1927.
The Jealous Gods; a processional novel of the fifth century B.C. (concerning one Alcibiades). Liveright, 1928.
Julia France and Her Times. Macmillan, 1912.
Life in the War Zone. System Printing, 1916.
The Living Present. Frederick A. Stokes, 1917.
Mrs. Balfame. Frederick A. Stokes, 1916.
Mrs. Pendleton's Four-in-hand. Macmillan, 1903.
My San Francisco, a Wayward Biography. Bobbs-Merrill, 1946.
Patience Sparhawk and Her Times. Lane, 1897.
Perch of the Devil. Frederick A. Stokes, 1914.
A Question of Time. Lovell, 1891.
Rezánov. Frederick A. Stokes, 1906.
Rezánov and Doña Concha. Frederick A. Stokes, 1937. (Includes *Rezánov* and the short story "Doña Concha," previously published under the title *Concha Arguello, Sister Dominica.*)
Rulers of Kings. Harper, 1904.
Senator North. Lane, 1900.
The Sisters-in-law; a novel of our time. Frederick A. Stokes, 1921.
Sleeping Fires. Frederick A. Stokes, 1922.
The Sophisticates. Liveright, 1931.
The Splendid Idle Forties; short stories of Old California. Macmillan, 1902. (Revised and enlarged edition of the 1894 edition of *Before the Gringo Came.*)
Tower of Ivory. Macmillan, 1910.
Transplanted. Dodd, 1919. (First published in 1898 as *American Wives and English Husbands.*)
The Travelling Thirds. Harper, 1905.
The Valiant Runaways; a book for boys. Dodd, Mead, 1898.
What Dreams May Come; a romance. By Frank Lin [pseud.]. Belford, Clarke, 1888.
A Whirl Asunder. Frederick A. Stokes, 1895.
The White Morning; a novel of the power of the German woman in wartime. Frederick A. Stokes, 1918.

AMBROSE BIERCE
The Ambrose Bierce Satanic Reader; selections from the invective journalism of the great satirist. Doubleday, 1968.
Ambrose Bierce: Selected Journalism from 1898–1901. Delmas Books, 1979. (Laurence I. Berkove, editor.)
Battle Sketches. First Edition Club, 1930.
Battlefields and Ghosts; after forty-odd years there are neither enemies nor victories, but only gracious mountains and sleepy valleys all aflame with autum foliage . . . hazy and dim as old memories. Harvest Press, 1931.
Black Beetles in Amber. Western Authors Publishing, 1892.
Can Such Be? Cassell, 1893.
Civil War. Gateway Editions, 1956.
Cobwebs: Being the Fables of Zambri, the Parsee. By Dod Grile [pseud.]. Routledge, 1874.
Collected Works. Neall, 1909-1912. 12 volumes.
Collected Writings of Ambrose Bierce. Citadel Press, 1946. (Introduction by Clifton Fadiman.)
The Complete Short Stories of Ambrose Bierce. Doubleday, 1970. Vol. 1: *The World of Humor;* Vol. 2: *The World of War and the World of Tall Tales.*
The Cynic's Word Book. Doubleday, Page, 1906.
The Dance of Death. By William Herman [pseud.]. Henry Keller, 1877.
The Devil's Dictionary. Dover, 1911. (Published in part in 1906 as *The Cynic's Word Book.*)
The Devil's Word Book. Rather Press, 1975.
The Enlarged Devil's Dictionary. Doubleday, 1967.
Fantastic Fables. Putnam's, 1899.
The Fiend's Delight. By Dod Grile [pseud.]. Luyster, 1873.

Ghost and Horror Stories. Dover, 1964. (Selected and introduced by E. F. Bleiler.)

A Horseman in the Sky. A Watcher by the Dead. The Man and the Snake. Book Club of San Francisco, 1920.

In the Midst of Life. Chatto & Windus, 1892. 2 volumes. Part 1: *Tales of Soldiers;* Part 2: *Tales of Civilians.* (Published in 1891 as *Tales of Soldiers and Civilians.*)

An Invocation. Printed for the Book Club of California by John Henry Nash, 1928.

Letters. Book Club of California, 1922. (Edited by B. C. Pope.)

The Lion and the Lamb. Archetype Press, 1939.

The Monk and the Hangman's Daughter. Schulte, 1892. (Co-author, Gustave Adolph Danzinger.)

Nuggets and Dust Panned Out in California. By Dod Grile [pseud.]. Chatto & Windus, 1873.

The Sardonic Humor of Ambrose Bierce. Dover, 1963. (Edited by George Barkin.)

The Shadow on the Dial, and Other Essays. A. M. Robertson, 1909.

Shapes of Clay. W. E. Wood, 1903.

A Son of the Gods, and, A Horseman in the Sky. P. Elder, 1907.

Stories and Fables of Ambrose Bierce. Stemmer House, 1977. (Edited by Edward Wagenknecht.)

Tales of Soldiers and Civilians. E. L. G. Steele, 1891.

Ten Tales. First Edition Club, 1925.

Twenty-one-Letters of Ambrose Bierce. G. Kirk, 1922.

Write It Right; a little blacklist of literary faults. Neale, 1909.

RICHARD BRAUTIGAN

The Abortion; an historical romance. Simon & Schuster, 1966.

All Watched Over By Machines of Loving Grace. Communications Company, 1967.

Confederate General from Big Sur. Grove, 1964.

Dreaming of Babylon; a private eye novel, 1942. Delacorte, 1977.

The Galilee Hitch-hiker. White Rabbit Press, 1958.

The Hawkline Monster; a Gothic western. Simon & Schuster, 1974.

In Watermelon Sugar. Four Seasons Foundation, 1968.

June Thirtieth, June Thirtieth. Delacorte, 1978.

Lay the Marble Tea; twenty-four poems. Carp Press, 1959.

Loading Mercury with a Pitchfork. Simon & Schuster, 1976.

The Octopus Frontier. Carp Press, 1960.

The Pill Versus the Springhill Mine Disaster. Four Seasons Foundation, 1968.

Revenge of the Lawn; stories, 1962-1970. Simon & Schuster, 1971.

Rommel Drives on Deep into Egypt. Delacorte, 1970.

Sombrero Fallout; a Japanese novel. Simon & Schuster, 1976.

Trout Fishing in America; a novel. Four Seasons Foundation, 1967.

Trout Fishing in America; The Pill Versus the Springhill Mine Disaster; and, In Watermelon Sugar. Delacorte, 1969.

Willard and His Bowling Trophies; a perverse mystery. Simon and Schuster, 1975.

DOROTHY BRYANT

The Comforter. Eran Press, 1973.

Ella Price's Journal; a novel. Lippincott, 1972.

The Garden of Eros; a novel. Ata Books, 1979.

The Kin of Ata Are Waiting for You. Random/Moon Books, 1976. (Formerly published as *The Comforter.*)

Miss Giardino. Ata Books, 1978.

Writing A Novel; some hints for beginners. Ata Books, 1978.

NIVEN BUSCH

The Actor. Simon & Schuster, 1955.

California Street. Simon & Schuster, 1959.

The Carrington Incident. Morrow, 1939.

Continent's End. Simon & Schuster, 1980.

Day of the Conquerors. Harper, 1946.

Duel in the Sun. Morrow, 1944.

The Furies. Dial, 1948.

The Gentleman from California. Simon & Schuster, 1965.

The Hate Merchant. Simon & Schuster, 1952.

The San Franciscans. Simon & Schuster, 1962.

The Takeover. Simon & Schuster, 1973.

They Dream of Home. Appleton, 1944.

Twenty-one Americans; being profiles of some people famous in our time, together with silly pictures of them. Doubleday, 1930.

HERB CAEN

Baghdad-by-the-Bay. Doubleday, 1949.

Baghdad, 1951. Doubleday, 1950.

The Cable Car and the Dragon. Doubleday, 1972. (For younger readers.)

Don't Call It Frisco. Doubleday, 1953.

Guide to San Francisco. Doubleday, 1957.

Herb Caen's San Francisco; the guide to the city and the Bay Area today. Doubleday, 1965.

New Guide to San Francisco and the Bay Area. Doubleday, 1958.

One Man's San Francisco. Doubleday, 1976.

Only in San Francisco. Doubleday, 1960.

The San Francisco Book. Houghton Mifflin, 1948.

San Francisco, City on Golden Hills. Doubleday, 1967. (Co-author, Dong Kingman.)

DON CARPENTER

Blade of Light. Harcourt, Brace and World, 1967.

A Couple of Comedians. Simon & Schuster, 1980.

Getting Off. Dutton, 1971.

Hard Rain Falling. Harcourt, Brace and World, 1966.

The Murder of the Frogs and Other Stories. Harcourt, Brace and World, 1969.

The True Life Story of Jody McKeegan. Dutton, 1975.

EVAN CONNELL

The Anatomy Lesson, and Other Stories. Viking, 1957.

At the Crossroads. Simon & Schuster, 1965.

The Connoisseur. Knopf, 1974.

The Diary of a Rapist. Simon & Schuster, 1966.

Double Honeymoon. Putnam, 1976.

A Long Desire. Holt, Rinehart, 1979.

Mr. Bridge. Knopf, 1969.

Mrs. Bridge. Viking, 1958.

Notes From a Bottle Found on the Beach at Carmel. Viking, 1963.

The Patriot. Viking, 1960.

Points for a Compass Rose. Knopf, 1973.

RICHARD HENRY DANA

An Autobiographical Sketch (1815–1842). Shoe String Press, 1953.

Cruelty to Seamen; being the case of Nichols and Couch. Private printing, 1937.

Journal. Harvard University Press, 1968. 3 volumes.

The Seaman's Friend. 1841.

Speeches in Stirring Times, and, Letters to a Son. Houghton Mifflin, 1910.

To Cuba and Back; a vacation voyage. Ticknor & Fields, 1859.

Two Years Before the Mast; a personal narrative of life at sea. Harper, 1840.

Usury Laws; their nature, expediency, and influence. Opinions of Jeremy Bentham and John Calvin, with review of the existing situation and recent experience of the United States, by Richard H. Dana, and others. The Society for Political Education, 1881.

LAWRENCE FERLINGHETTI

After the Cry of the Birds. Dave Haselwood, 1967.

Back Roads to Far Places. New Directions, 1971.

Berlin. Golden Mountain Press, 1961.

A Coney Island of the Mind; poems. New Directions, 1958.

An Eye on the World; selected poems. MacGibbon & Kee, 1967.

Her. New Directions, 1960.

Landscapes of Living and Dying. New Directions, 1979.

Love Is No Stone on the Moon; an automatic poem. Arif Press, 1971.

The Mexican Night; travel journal. New Directions, 1970.

Moscow in the Wilderness: Segovia in the Snow. Beach Books, 1967.

Northwest Ecolog. City Lights, 1978.

The Old Italians Dying. City Lights, 1976.

Open Eye. Sun Books, 1972. (Includes *Open Head* by Allen Ginsberg.)

Open Eye, Open Heart. New Directions, 1973.

Pictures of the Gone World. City Lights, 1955.

A Political Pamphlet. Anarchist Resistance Press, 1976.

Routines; short plays. New Directions, 1964.

The Secret Meaning of Things. New Directions, 1969.

Starting From San Francisco. New Directions, 1961; 1967 (revised and enlarged.)

Tentative Description of a Dinner Given to Promote the Impeachment of President Eisenhower. Golden Mountain Press, 1958.

To Fuck Is To Love Again; Kurie [sic] Eleison Keristas, or, The Situation in the West, Followed by a Holy Proposal. Fuck You Press, 1965.

Tyrannus Nix? New Directions, 1969.

Unfair Arguments with Existence; seven plays for a new theatre. New Directions, 1963.

Who Are We Now? New Directions, 1976.

KATHRYN FORBES

Mama's Bank Account. Harcourt, 1943.

Transfer Point. Harcourt, 1947.

ERNEST J. GAINES

The Autobiography of Miss Jane Pittman. Dial, 1971.

Bloodline. Dial, 1968.

Catherine Carmier. Atheneum, 1964.

In My Father's House. Knopf, 1978.

A Long Day in November. Dial, 1971. (A short story for younger readers.)

Of Love and Dust. Dial, 1967.

HENRY GEORGE

Addresses. Henry George Foundation, 1936-1938. (4 volumes in 1: *The Crime of Poverty; Moses; The Study of Political Economy; Thy Kingdom Come.*)

The Complete Works of Henry George. Fels Fund Library Edition, Doubleday, Page, 1906-1911. 10 volumes.

The Condition of Labour; an open letter to Pope Leo XIII, with appendices containing the encyclical of Pope Leo XIII on the condition of labour, Dr. Edward McGlynn's statement, and Bishop Nulty's essay on the land question. Henry George Fund of Great Britain, 1934.

The Irish Land Question; what it involves, and how alone it can be settled. An appeal to the land leagues. Appleton, 1881.

The Land Question, Property in Land, The Condition of Labor. Robert Schalkenbach Foundation, 1935. (*The Land Question* was first published as *The Irish Land Question.*)

Our Land and Land Policy, National and State. White & Bauer, 1871.

Our Land and Land Policy; speeches, lectures and miscellaneous writings. Doubleday & McClure, 1902.

A Perplexed Philosopher; being an examination of Mr. Herbert Spencer's various utterances on the land question with some incidental reference to his Synthetic Philosophy. Webster, 1892.

Progress and Poverty; an inquiry into the causes of industrial depressions and of increase of want with increase of wealth — the remedy. W. M. Hinton, 1879.

Property in Land. A passage-at-arms between the Duke of Argyll and Henry George. Webster, 1893. (Co-author, George Douglas Campbell Argyll.)

Protection or Fair Trade; an examination of the tariff question, with especial regard to the interests of labor. H. George, 1886.

Science of Political Economy. Doubleday & McClure, 1898.

Social Problems. National Single Tax League, c.1883.

HERBERT GOLD

The Age of Happy Problems. Dial, 1962.

Biafra Goodbye. Twowindows Press, 1970.

Birth of a Hero. Viking, 1951.

Fathers; a novel in the form of a memoir. Random, 1967. (To be reissued in 1980 by Creative Arts Book Company.)

The Great American Jackpot. Random, 1969.

He/She. Arbor House, 1980.

Love and Like. Dial, 1960. (Short stories.)

The Magic Will; stories and essays of a decade. Random, 1971.

The Man Who Was Not With It. Little, Brown, 1956. (Published as *The Wild Life* by Permabooks, 1957.)

My Last Two Thousand Years. Random, 1972.

The Optimist. Little, Brown, 1959.

The Prospect Before Us. World, 1954. (Published as *Room Clerk* by New American Library, 1956.)

Salt; a novel. Dial, 1963.

Slave Trade. Arbor House, 1979.

Swiftie the Magician. McGraw-Hill, 1974.

Therefore Be Bold. Dial, 1960.

Waiting For Cordelia. Arbor House, 1977.

The Young Prince and the Magic Cone. Doubleday, 1973. (For younger readers.)

DASHIELL HAMMETT

The Adventures of Sam Spade, and Other Stories. Spivak, 1944. (Republished by Spivak in 1949 as *They Can Only Hang You Once.*)

The Big Knockover; selected stories and short novels. Random, 1966. (Edited by Lillian Hellman. Published in England as *The Dashiell Hammett Story Omnibus*, Cassell, 1966.)

The Complete Dashiell Hammett. Knopf, 1942.

The Continental Op. Spivak, 1945.

The Continental Op; more stories from "The Big Knockover." Dell, 1967.

The Continental Op. Random, 1974. (Edited by Steven Marcus. Contains different stories from the previous collections with the same title.)

Creeping Siamese; a Dashiell Hammett detective. Spivak, 1950.

The Dain Curse. Knopf, 1929.

Dashiell Hammett Omnibus: Red Harvest; The Dain Curse; The Maltese Falcon. Knopf, 1935.

Dead Yellow Women. Spivak, 1947.

The Glass Key. Knopf, 1931.

Hammett Homicides. Spivak, 1946.

The Maltese Falcon. Knopf, 1930.

The Maltese Falcon, and, The Thin Man. Vintage, 1964.

A Man Called Spade. Dell, 1945.

A Man Named Thin, and Other Stories. Joseph W. Ferman, 1962.

Nightmare Town. Spivak, 1948.

Novels of Dashiell Hammett. Knopf, 1965 (revised edition).

$106,000 Blood Money. Spivak, 1943. (Published as *Blood Money*, Dell, 1944, and as *The Big Knockover*, Jonathan Press, 1948.)

Red Harvest. Knopf, 1929.

The Return of the Continental Op. Spivak, 1945.

The Thin Man. Knopf, 1934.

Woman in the Dark. Spivak. 1951.

BRET HARTE

The Adventures of Padre Vicentio; a legend of San Francisco. W. E. Bentley, 1939.

Ah, Sin. A dramatic work by Mark Twain and Bret Harte. Book Club of California, 1961. (Edited by Frederick Anderson.)

Ancestors of Peter Atherly, and Other Tales. Houghton Mifflin, 1900.

The Argonauts of North Liberty. Houghton Mifflin, 1888.

Barker's Luck, and Other Stories. Houghton Mifflin, 1896.

The Bell-Ringer of Angel's, and Other Stories. Houghton Mifflin, 1894.

Berkeley, Xanadu of the San Francisco Bay. Hart Press, 1951.

The Best of Bret Harte. Houghton Mifflin, 1947.

The Best Short Stories of Bret Harte. Modern Library, 1947.

Bret Harte's Stories of the Old West. Houghton Mifflin, 1940.

By Shore and Sedge. Houghton Mifflin, 1885.

Captain Jim's Friend, and, The Argonauts of North Liberty. Tauchnitz, 1889.

Clarence. Houghton Mifflin, 1895.

Colonel Starbottle's Client, and Some Other People. Houghton Mifflin, 1892.

Condensed Novels, and Other Papers. Carleton, 1867.

Condensed Novels, Second Series: New Burlesques. Houghton Mifflin, 1902.

Cressy. Houghton Mifflin, 1889.

The Crusade of the "Excelsior"; a novel. Houghton Mifflin, 1887.

Dickens in Camp. Howell, 1922. (Printed by Edwin Grabhorn.)

Drift From Two Shores. Houghton, Osgood, 1878.

East and West; poems. Osgood, 1871.

Echoes of the Foothills. Osgood, 1875.

An Episode of Fiddletown, and Other Sketches. Routledge, 1873.

Excelsior. Donaldson Brothers (printers), 1877 (?).

Fables, by G. Washington Æsop [pseud.] and Bret Harte. Hamilton, 1882.

A First Family of Tasajura. Macmillan (London), 1891; Houghton Mifflin, 1892.

Flip, and Found at Blazing Star. Houghton Mifflin, 1882.

The Fool of Five Forks. Routledge, 1875.

From Sand Hill to Pine. Houghton Mifflin, 1900.

Frontier Stories. Houghton Mifflin, 1887.

Gabriel Conroy. American Publishing Company, 1876.

The Heathen Chinee. Western News, 1870.

An Heiress of Red Dog, and Other Sketches. Tauchnitz, 1879.

Her Letter, His Answer, and Her Last Letter. Houghton Mifflin, 1905.

The Heritage of Dedlow Marsh, and Other Tales. Houghton Mifflin, 1889.

The Hoodlum Band, and Other Stories. Ward, Lock, 1878. (English edition; published in the United States as *Drift From Two Shores.*)

How Santa Claus Came to Simpson's Bar. Ward Ritchie Press, 1941.

Idyls of the Foothills; in prose and verse. Tauchnitz, 1874.

In a Hollow of the Hills. Houghton Mifflin, 1895.

In the Carquinez Woods. Longmans, Green, 1883.

Jeff Briggs' Love Story, and Other Sketches. Chatto & Windus, 1880.

Jinny. Routledge, 1878.

The Lectures of Bret Harte; compiled from various sources, to which is added "The Piracy of Bret Harte's Fables" by Charles Meeker Kozlay. Kozlay, 1909.

The Letters of Bret Harte. Houghton Mifflin, 1926. (Assembled and edited by Geoffrey Bret Harte.)

The Lost Galleon and Other Tales. Towne & Bacon, 1867.

Lothaw; or, The Adventures of a young gentleman in search of a religion, by Mr. Benjamins (i.e. Bret Harte). J. C. Hotten, 1871 (?).

Luck of Roaring Camp, and Other Sketches. Fields, Osgood, 1871.

The Man on the Beach. Routledge, 1878.

Maruja. Houghton Mifflin, 1885.

A Millionaire of Rough-and-Ready, and Devil's Ford. Houghton Mifflin, 1887.

Mr. Jack Hamlin's Mediation, and Other Stories. Houghton Mifflin, 1899.

Mrs. Skagg's Husbands, and Other Sketches. Osgood, 1873.

M'liss; an idyll of Red Mountain. A story of California in 1863. Robert M. DeWitt, 1873.

My Friend the Tramp. Routledge, 1877 (?).

The Niece of Snapshot Harry's, Trent's Trust, and Other Stories; glossary and index to characters. Houghton Mifflin, 1921.

A Night at Wingdam; together with a letter from the author to Dr. J. L. Ver Mehr. California Literary Pamphlets, Plantin Press, 1936.

On the Frontier. Houghton Mifflin, 1884.

Openings in the Old Trail. Houghton Mifflin, 1902.

The Outcasts of Poker Flat. 1869.

A Phyllis of the Sierras, and, A Drift From Redwood Camp. Houghton Mifflin, 1888.

Poems. Osgood, 1871.

The Poetical Works of Bret Harte; including the drama of "The Two Men of Sandy Bar." Houghton, Mifflin, 1887.

Prose and Poetry. Routledge, 1873 (?).

A Protégée of Jack Hamlin's, and Other Stories. Houghton Mifflin, 1894.

The Queen of the Pirate Isle. Chatto & Windus, 1886. (Illustrated by Kate Greenaway.)

The Right Eye of the Commander; a New Year's legend of Spanish California. W. & E. Bentley, 1937.

Sally Dows, and Other Stories. Houghton Mifflin, 1893.

Salomy Jane. Houghton Mifflin, 1910.

Salomy Jane's Kiss. Revised and elaborated version of the famous story. Grosset & Dunlap, 1915.

San Francisco in 1866; being letters to the Springfield Republican. Book Club of San Francisco, 1951.

A Sappho of Green Springs, and Other Stories. Houghton Mifflin, 1891.

The Select Works of Bret Harte, in Prose and Poetry. Chatto & Windus, 188?.

Sensation Novels, Condensed. J. C. Hotten, 1871.

Sketches of the Sixties; being forgotten material now collected for the first time from the Californian, 1864-1867. J. Howell, 1926. (Co-author, Mark Twain.)

Snow-bound at Eagle's. Houghton Mifflin, 1886.

Some Later Verses. Chatto & Windus, 1898.

Stories and Poems, and Other Uncollected Writings; compiled by Charles Meeker Kozlay, with an introductory account of Harte's early contributions to the California press. Houghton Mifflin, 1914.

Stories in Light and Shadow. Houghton Mifflin, 1898.

Stories of the Early West, The Luck of Roaring Camp, and Sixteen Other Exciting Tales of Mining and Frontier Days. Platt & Munk, 1964.

Stories of the Sierra and Other Sketches; with a story of wild western life by Joaquin Miller. J. C. Hotten, 1872.

The Story of a Mine. Osgood, 1878.

The Story of Enriquez; Chu Chu; The Devotion of Enriquez; The Passing of Enriquez. Printed by Edwin and Robert Grabhorn, 1924.

Sue; a play in three acts. Greening, 1902. (Co-author, T. Edgar Pemberton.)

Susy; a story of the plains. Houghton Mifflin, 1893.

Tales of the Argonauts, and Other Sketches. Osgood, 1875.

Tales of the Gold Rush. Heritage Press, 1944. (Introduction by Oscar Lewis.)

Tales of the West. Nelson, 1928.

Tales of Trail and Town. Houghton Mifflin, 1898.

Tales, Poems, and Sketches. Cassell, 1887.

Tennessee's Partner. P. Elder, 1907.

Thankful Blossom; a romance of the Jerseys, 1779. Osgood, 1877.

That Heathen Chinee and Other Poems, Mostly Humorous. J. C. Hotten, 1871 (?).

Three Partners; or, the big strike on Heavy Tree Hill. Houghton Mifflin, 1897.

Trent's Trust, and Other Stories. Houghton Mifflin, 1903.

Truthful James and Other Poems. Routledge, n.d.

The Twins of Table Mountain, and Othe Stories. Houghton, Osgood, 1879.

Two Men of Sandy Bar; a drama. Osgood, 1876.

Under the Redwoods. Houghton Mifflin, 1901.

A Waif of the Plains. Houghton Mifflin, 1890.

Wan Lee, The Pagan, and Other Sketches. Routledge, 1876 (?).

A Ward of the Golden Gate. Houghton Mifflin, 1890.

The Wild West; stories. Harrison, 1930.

The Writings of Bret Harte. Houghton Mifflin, 1890-1912. 20 volumes.

WARREN HINCKLE

Guerilla War in the USA. 1971.

If You Have a Lemon, Make Lemonade. Putnam, 1974.

The Richest Place on Earth; the story of Virginia City, Nevada, and the heyday of the Comstock Lode. Houghton Mifflin, 1978.

The Ten-Second Jailbreak. Holt, 1973.

ERIC HOFFER

Before the Sabbath. Harper & Row, 1979.

First Things, Last Things. Harper & Row, 1971.

In Our Time. Harper & Row, 1976.

The Ordeal of Change. Harper & Row, 1963.

The Passionate State of Mind, and Other Aphorisms. Harper & Row, 1955.

Reflections on the Human Condition. Harper & Row, 1973.

The Temper of Our Time. Harper & Row, 1967.

The True Believer; thoughts on the nature of mass movements. Harper & Row, 1951.

Working and Thinking on the Waterfront; a journal, June 1958-May 1959. Harper & Row, 1969.

HELEN HOLDREDGE

Firebelle Lillie. Meredith Press, 1967.

The House of the Strange Woman. Nourse, 1961.

Mammy Pleasant. Putnam, 1953.

Mammy Pleasant's Partner. Putnam, 1954.

The Woman in Black; the life of Lola Montez. Putnam, 1955.

JACK KEROUAC

Big Sur. Farrar, Straus, 1962.

Book of Dreams. City Lights, 1961.

Desolation Angels; a novel. Coward, McCann, 1965.

The Dharma Bums. Viking, 1958.

Dr. Sax; Faust part three. Grove, 1959.

Excerpts from Visions of Cody. New Directions, 1959.

Heaven and Other Poems. Grey Fox, 1977.

Lonesome Traveler. McGraw, 1960.
Maggie Cassidy; a novel. Avon, 1959.
Mexico City Blues. Grove, 1959.
On the Road. Viking, 1957.
Pic. Grove, 1971.
Pull My Daisy; text ad-libbed by Jack Kerouac for the film by Robert Frank and Alfred Leslie. Grove, 1961.
Rimbaud. City Lights, 1960.
Satori in Paris. Grove, 1966.
Scattered Poems. City Lights, 1971.
The Scripture of the Golden Eternity. Totem Press, 1960.
Subterraneans. Grove, 1958.
The Town and the City. Harcourt, 1950.
Tristessa. Avon, 1960. (Published in England with *Visions of Gerard* by Deutsch, 1964.)
Vanity of Duluoz; an adventurous education, 1935-1946. Coward, McCann, 1968.
Visions of Cody. New Directions, 1960. (Introduction by Allen Ginsberg.)
Visions of Gerard. Farrar, Straus, 1963.

THEODORA KROEBER

Alfred Kroeber; a personal configuration. University of California Press, 1970.
Almost Ancestors; the first Californians. Sierra Club, 1968. (Co-author, Robert Heizer.)
Carrousel. Atheneum, 1977. (For younger readers.)
Inland Whale; nine stories retold from California Indian legends. Indiana University Press, 1959.
Ishi in Two Worlds; a biography of the last wild Indian in North America. University of California Press, 1961.
Ishi, Last of His Tribe. Parnassus, 1964.

C. Y. LEE

Cripple Mah and the New Order. Farrar, Straus, 1961.
Days of the Tong Wars. Ballantine Books, 1974.
The Flower Drum Song. Farrar, Straus, 1957.
Land of the Golden Mountain. Meredith Press, 1967.
Lover's Point. Farrar, Straus, 1958.
Madame Goldenflower. Farrar, Straus, 1960.
The Sawbwa and His Secretary; my Burmese reminiscences. Farrar, Straus, 1959. (Published in England as *Corner of Heaven;* my Burmese reminiscences, by W. H. Allen, 1960.)
The Virgin Market. Doubleday, 1964.

ELLA LEFFLAND

Love Out of Season. Atheneum, 1974.
Mrs. Munck. Houghton Mifflin, 1970.
Rumors of Peace. Harper & Row, 1979.

OSCAR LEWIS

Bay Window Bohemia; an account of the brilliant artistic world of gaslit San Francisco. Doubleday, 1956.
The Big Four; the story of Huntington, Stanford, Hopkins, and Crocker, and of the building of the Central Pacific. Knopf, 1938.
Bonanza Inn; America's first luxury hotel. Knopf, 1939. (Co-author, Carroll D. Hall.)
California Heritage. Crowell, 1949.
The California Mining Towns; a series of twelve rare early views of towns and camps of the gold rush; text by Oscar Lewis. Book Club of California. 1933-1934.
Fabulous San Simeon; a history of the Hearst Castle, a California State Monument located on the scenic coast of California, together with a guide to the treasures on display. California Historical Society, 1958.
A Family of Builders; the story of the Haases and Thompsons, California pioneers since gold rush days. Privately printed (Grabhorn Press), 1961.
Fine Printing in the Far West. Platen Press, 1946.
George Davidson, Pioneer West Coast Scientist. University of California Press, 1954.
Hawaii, Gem of the Pacific. Random, 1954. (For younger readers.)
Hearn and His Biographers; the record of a literary controversy. Westgate Press, 1930.
Here Lived the Californians. Rinehart, 1957.
High Sierra Country. Duell, Sloan, and Pearce, 1955.
I Remember Christine. Knopf, 1942.
Lola Montez; the mid-Victorian bad girl in California. Colt, 1938.
The Lost Years; a biographical fantasy. Knopf, 1951.
One Fifty-five Sansome; being the story of the land on which the Industrial Indemnity Building stands today. Publisher and date uncertain.
The Origin of the Celebrated Jumping Frog of Calaveras County. Book Club of California, 1931.
The Sacramento River. Holt, Rinehart, and Winston, 1970. (For younger readers.)
Sagebrush Casinos; the story of legal gambling in California. Doubleday, 1953.
San Francisco: Mission to Metropolis. Howell-North, 1966.
San Francisco Since 1872; a pictorial history of seven decades. 1946. (Photographs and poems from the collection of Milton S. Ray; historical text by Oscar Lewis.)
Sea Routes to the Gold Fields; the migration by water to California in 1849-1852. Knopf, 1949.
Silver Kings; the lives and times of Mackay, Fair, Flood, and O'Brien, lords of the Nevada Comstock Lode. Knopf, 1947.
The Story of California. Garden City Books, 1955. (For younger readers.)
The Story of Oregon. Garden City Books, 1957. (For younger readers.)

Sutter's Fort; gateway to the gold fields. Prentice-Hall, 1966.
This Was San Francisco; being a first-hand account of the evolution of one of America's favorite cities. (Compiled and edited by Oscar Lewis.) David McKay, 1962.
To Remember Albert M. (Mickey) Bender; notes for a biography. Grabhorn/Hoyem, 1953.
The Town That Died Laughing; the story of Austin, Nevada, rambunctious early-day mining camp, and of its renowned newspaper, The Reese River Reveille. Little, Brown, 1955.
The Tree; a California story. Oscar Lewis and Andrew Hoyem, 1976.
The Uncertain Journey. Knopf, 1945.
The War in the Far West: 1861-1865. Doubleday, 1961.
Within the Golden Gate; a survey of the history, resources, and points of interest in the Bay Region prepared for delegates to the United Nations Conference on International Organizations. San Francisco Bay Area Council, 1945.
The Wonderful City of Carrie Van Wie; paintings of San Francisco at the turn of the century. Grabhorn Press for the Book Club of California, 1963. (Text by Oscar Lewis.)

JACK LONDON

The Abysmal Brute. Century, 1913.
The Acorn-planter; a California forest play planned to be sung by efficient singers, accompanied by a capable orchestra. Macmillan, 1916.
Adventure. Macmillan, 1911.
The Apostate. C. H. Kerr, 1919(?).
The Assassination Bureau, Ltd. McGraw-Hill, 1963. (Completed by Robert L. Fish from notes by Jack London.)
Before Adam. Macmillan, 1907.
The Best Short Stories of Jack London. Sun Dial, 1945.
The Bodley Head Jack London. Bodley Head, 1963-1964. 2 volumes.
Brown Wolf, and Other Jack London Stories. Macmillan, 1966, c1920.
Burning Daylight. Macmillan, 1910.
Call of the Wild. Macmillan, 1903.
Children of the Frost. Macmillan, 1902.
Cruise of the Dazzler. Century, 1902.
Cruise of the Snark. Macmillan, 1911.
Curious Fragments; Jack London's tales of fantasy fiction. Kennikat Press, 1975.
A Daughter of the Snows. Lippincott, 1902.
Daughters of the Rich; a play. Holmes Book Company, 1971, c1915. (With a chronological bibliography of Jack London's plays, compiled by James E. Sisson.)
The Dream of Debs; a story of industrial revolt. C. H. Kerr, 192?.
Dutch Courage and Other Stories. Macmillan, 1922.
Faith of Men, and Other Stories. Macmillan, 1904.
The Game. Macmillan, 1905.
God of His Fathers, and Other Stories. McClure, Phillips, 1901.

Gold; a play in three acts. Holmes Book Company, 1972. (Co-author, Herbert Heron; edited by James E. Sisson.)

Goliath; a Utopian fantasy. Thorp Springs Press, 1973. (First published in ''Red Magazine'' (England) and later collected in *Revolution and Other Essays.*)

Great Short Works of Jack London; Call of the Wild, White Fang, and six stories. Harper & Row, 1965. (Edited by Earle Labor.)

Hearts of Three. Mills & Boon, 1918.

House of Pride, and Other Tales of Hawaii. Macmillan, 1912.

The Human Drift. Macmillan, 1917.

The Iron Heel. Macmillan, 1908.

Jack London, American Rebel; a collection of his social writings together with an extensive study of the man and his time. Citadel Press, 1947. (Edited by Philip S. Foner.)

Jack London Reports; war correspondence, sports articles, and miscellaneous writings. Doubleday, 1970.

Jack London's Articles and Short Stories in the (Oakland) High School Aegis. The London Collector, no. 3, 1971. (Edited and introduced by James E. Sisson.)

Jack London's Tales of Adventure. Hanover House, 1956. (Edited by Irving Shepard.)

Jack London's ''What Life Means To Me;'' memorial edition. C. H. Kerr, 1916.

Jerry of the Islands. Macmillan, 1917.

John Barleycorn. Century, 1913.

The Kempton-Wace Letters. Macmillan, 1903. (Co-author, Anna Strunsky.)

Letters From Jack London; containing an unpublished correspondence between London and Sinclair Lewis. Odyssey, 1965. (Edited by King Hendricks and Irving Shepard.)

The Little Lady of the Big House. Macmillan, 1916.

London's Essays of Revolt. Vanguard Press, 1926.

Lost Face. Macmillan, 1910.

Love of Life, and Other Stories. Macmillan, 1907.

Martin Eden. Macmillan, 1909.

Michael, Brother of Jerry. Macmillan, 1917. (Sequel to *Jerry of the Islands.*)

Moon-face, and Other Stories. Macmillan, 1906.

Mutiny of the Elsinore. Macmillan, 1914.

The Night-born. Century, 1913.

On the Makaloa Mat. Macmillan, 1919.

The People of the Abyss. Macmillan, 1903.

The Red One. Macmillan, 1918.

Revolution, and Other Essays. Macmillan, 1910.

The Road. Macmillan, 1907.

The Scarlet Plague. Macmillan, 1915.

The Scab. C. H. Kerr, 190?. (No. 44 in the *Pocket Library of Socialism.*)

The Science Fiction of Jack London; an anthology. Gregg, 1975. (Edited by Richard G. Powers.)

Scorn of Women; in three acts. Macmillan, 1906.

The Sea Wolf. Macmillan, 1904.

Short Stories. Hill & Wang, 1960.

Smoke Bellew. Century, 1912.

Son of the Sun. Doubleday, 1912. (Published as *The Adventures of Captain Grief* in 1954, World Publishing.)

The Son of the Wolf; tales of the Far North. Houghton Mifflin, 1900.

South Sea Tales. Macmillan, 1911.

Star Rover. Macmillan, 1915.

Stories of Hawaii. Appleton-Century, 1965.

The Strength of the Strong. C. H. Kerr, 1912.

The Sun-Dog Trail, and Other Stories. World, 1951.

Tales of the Fish Patrol. Macmillan, 1905.

Theft; a play in four acts. Macmillan, 1910.

Thirteen Tales of Terror. Popular Library, 1978.

Turtles of Tasman. Macmillan, 1916.

The Valley of the Moon. Macmillan, 1913.

War of the Classes. Macmillan, 1905.

When God Laughs, and Other Stories. Macmillan, 1911.

White Fang. Macmillan, 1906.

The Works of Jack London. McKinley, Stone & MacKenzie, 1906. 12 volumes.

FRANK NORRIS

The Argonaut Manuscript Limited Edition of Frank Norris's Works. Doubleday, Doran, 1928. 10 volumes.

Blix. Doubleday & McClure, 1899.

Complete Works. Doubleday, Page, 1903. 10 volumes. (*Collected Writings,* from which the excerpt in this book is taken, is vol. 10.)

Deal in Wheat and Other Stories of the New and Old West. Doubleday, Page, 1903.

Frank Norris of ''The Wave;'' stories and sketches from the San Francisco weekly, 1893 to 1897. Westgate, 1931. (Introduction by Oscar Lewis; foreword by Charles Norris.)

The Joyous Miracle; a parable of Christmas. Doubleday, Page, 1906.

The Letters of Frank Norris. Book Club of California, 1956.

Literary Criticism. University of Texas Press, 1964. (Edited by Donald Pizer.)

A Man's Woman. Doubleday & McClure, 1900.

McTeague; a story of San Francisco. Doubleday & McClure, 1899.

Moran of the Lady Letty; a story of adventure off the California coast. Doubleday & McClure, 1898.

A Novelist in the Making; a collection of student themes, and the novels *Blix,* and *Vandover and the Brute.* Harvard University Press, 1970. (Edited by James D. Hart.)

The Octopus; a story of California. Doubleday, Page, 1901.

The Pit; a story of Chicago. Doubleday, Page, 1903.

Responsibilities of the Novelist, and Other Literary Essays. Doubleday, Page, 1903.

Six Essays on the Responsibilities of the Novelist. Alicat Bookshop Press, 1949.

The Third Circle. J. Lane, 1909.

Vandover and the Brute. Doubleday, Page, 1914.

Yvernelle; a legend of feudal France. Lippincott, 1892.

KATHLEEN NORRIS

The American Flaggs. Doubleday, Doran, 1936.

Angel in the House. Doubleday, Doran, 1922.

An Apple for Eve. Doubleday, Doran, 1942.

April Escapade. J. Murray, 1941.

Baker's Dozen. Arnow, 1938.

Barberry Bush. Doubleday, Page, 1927.

Beauty and the Beast. Doubleday, Doran, 1928.

Beauty in Letters. Doubleday, Doran, 1930.

Beauty's Daughter. Doubleday, Doran, 1935.

Belle-Mère. Doubleday, Doran, 1931.

Beloved Woman. Doubleday, Page, 1921.

The Best of Kathleen Norris. Hanover House, 1955.

The Black Flemings. Doubleday, 1926.

Bread into Roses. Doubleday, Doran, 1937.

Burned Fingers. Doubleday, Doran, 1945.

Butterfly. Doubleday, Page, 1923.

The Callahans and the Murphys. Heinemann, 1924.

Certain People of Importance. Doubleday, Page, 1922.

Christmas Eve. J. Murray, 1949.

Come Back to Me Beloved. Sun Dial, 1942.

Corner of Heaven. Doubleday, Doran, 1943.

Dedications. Printed for Charles G. Norris on the hand press of Wilder and Ellen Bentley, 1936.

Dina Cashman. Doubleday, Doran, 1942.

Family Gathering. Doubleday, 1959.

The Foolish Virgin. Doubleday, Doran, 1928.

The Fun of Being a Mother. Doubleday, Page, 1927.

Hands Full of Living; talks with American women. Doubleday, 1931.

Harriet and the Piper. Doubleday, Page, 1920.

The Heart of Rachael. Grosset & Dunlap, 1916.

Heartbroken Melody. Collier, 1938.

High Holiday. Doubleday, Doran, 1949.

Hildegarde. Doubleday, Page, 1926.

Home. Dutton, 1928.

Josselyn's Wife. Doubleday, 1918.

The Kelly Kid; a comedy in one act. Walter H. Baker, 1926. (Co-author, Dan Totheroh.)

Little Ships. Doubleday, Page, 1925.

Lost Sunrise. Doubleday, Doran, 1939.

Love Calls the Tune. Sun Dial, 1944.

The Love of Julie Borel. Doubleday, Doran, 1931.

The Lucky Lawrences. Doubleday, Doran, 1930.

Lucretia Lombard. Doubleday, Page, 1922.

Maiden Voyage. Doubleday, Doran, 1934.

Manhattan Love Song. Doubleday, Doran, 1934.

Margaret Yorke. Doubleday, Doran, 1930.

Martie, the Unconquered. Doubleday, Page, 1917.

Mink Coat. Doubleday, 1946.

Miss Harriet Townsend. Doubleday, 1955.

Morning Light. Doubleday, 1950.

Mother, a Story. Grosset & Dunlap, 1911.

Mother and Son. Dutton, 1929.

My Best Girl. Burt, 1927.

My California. Doubleday, Doran, 1933.

My San Francisco. Doubleday, Doran, 1932.

Mystery House. Doubleday, Doran, 1939.

Mystery of Pine Point. J. Murray, 1936.

Noon; an autobiographical sketch. Doubleday, Page, 1925.

One Nation Indivisible; a poem. Doubleday, Doran, 1942.

Over at the Crowley's. Doubleday, 1946.

Passion Flower. Burt, 1930.

Poor, Dear Margaret Kirby, and Other Stories. Grosset & Dunlap, 1913.

Red Silence. Doubleday, Doran, 1929.

The Rich Mrs. Burgoyne. Macmillan, 1912.

Rose of the World. Burt, 1924.

The Runaway. Doubleday, Doran, 1939.

Saturday's Child. Grosset & Dunlap, 1914.

The Sea Gull. Doubleday, Page, 1927.

Secondhand Wife. Doubleday, Doran, 1932.

Secret Marriage. Doubleday, Doran, 1936.

The Secret of the Marshbanks. Doubleday, Doran, 1940.

The Secrets of Hillyard House. Doubleday, 1947.

Shadow Marriage. Doubleday, 1952.

Shining Windows. Doubleday, Doran, 1935.

Sisters. Doubleday, Page, 1919.

Star-spangled Christmas. Doubleday, 1942.

Storm House. Doubleday, Doran, 1929.

The Story of Julia Page. Doubleday, Page, 1915.

These I Like Best; the favorite novels and stories of Kathleen Norris, chosen by herself. Doubleday, Doran, 1941.

Three Men and Diana. Doubleday, Doran, 1934.

Through a Glass Darkly. Doubleday, 1957.

The Treasure, and Undertow; two complete novels. Garden City Publishing, 1937.

Treehaven. Doubleday, Doran, 1932.

Undertow. Doubleday, Page, 1917.

The Venables. Doubleday, Doran, 1941.

Victoria; a play in four acts and twelve scenes. Doubleday, Doran, 1934.

Walls of Gold. Doubleday, 1933.

What Do You Want To See? Standard Oil Company of California, 1929.

What Price Peace? A handbook of peace for American women. Doubleday, Doran, 1928.

Wife for Sale. Doubleday, Doran, 1933.

Woman in Love. Doubleday, Doran, 1935.

The World Is Like That. Doubleday, Doran, 1940.

You Can't Have Everything. Doubleday, Doran, 1937.

The Younger Sister. Doubleday, Doran, 1932.

TILLIE OLSEN

Silences. Delacorte, 1978.

Tell Me a Riddle. Lippincott, 1961.

Yonnondio: From the Thirties. Delacorte, 1974.

JOSIAH ROYCE

Basic Writings of Josiah Royce. University of Chicago Press. 1968. 2 volumes. (Edited by John J. McDermott.)

California, From the Conquest in 1846 to the Second Vigilance Committee in San Francisco, 1856; a study of American character. Houghton Mifflin, 1886.

Conception of God; a philosophical discussion concerning the nature of the divine idea as a demonstrable reality, with Joseph LeConte, G. H. Howison, and Sidney Edward Mezes. Macmillan, 1897.

Conception of Immortality. Houghton Mifflin, 1900.

The Feud of Oakfield Creek; a novel of California life. Houghton Mifflin, 1887.

Fugitive Essays. Harvard University Press, 1920.

Herbert Spencer; an estimate and a review. Fox, Duffield, 1904.

Hope of the Great Community. Macmillan, 1916.

Lectures on Modern Idealism. Yale University Press, 1919.

The Letters of Josiah Royce. University of Chicago Press, 1970. (Edited by John Clendenning.)

Logical Essays. W. C. Brown, 1951.

Outlines of Psychology; an elementary treatise, with some practical application. Macmillan, 1903.

The Philosophy of Josiah Royce. Crowell, 1971.

The Philosophy of Loyalty. Macmillan, 1908.

Primer of Logical Analysis; for the use of composition students. Bancroft, 1881.

Principles of Logic. Wisdom Library, 1961.

The Problem of Christianity; lectures delivered at the Crowell Institute in Boston and at Manchester College, Oxford. Macmillan, 1913. 2 volumes.

Race Questions, Provincialism, and Other American Problems. Macmillan, 1908.

The Religious Aspect of Philosophy; a critique of the bases of conduct and of faith. Houghton Mifflin, 1885.

The Religious Philosophy of Josiah Royce. Syracuse University Press, 1952. (Edited by Stuart G. Brown.)

The Social Philosophy of Josiah Royce. Syracuse University Press, 1950. (Edited by Stuart G. Brown.)

The Sources of Religious Insight. Scribner's, 1912.

The Spirit of Modern Philosophy; an essay in the form of lectures. Houghton Mifflin, 1892.

Studies of Good and Evil; a series of essays upon problems of philosophy and life. Appleton, 1898.

War and Insurance. Macmillan, 1914.

William James, and Other Essays on the Philosophy of Life. Macmillan, 1911.

The World and the Individual. First Series: The Four Historical Conceptions of Being. Macmillan, 1899.

The World and the Individual. Second Series: Nature, Man, and the Moral Order. Macmillan, 1901.

WILLIAM SAROYAN

An Act or Two of Foolish Kindness. Penmaen Press, 1977.

The Adventures of Wesley Jackson. Harcourt, 1946.

After Thirty Years: The Daring Young Man on the Flying Trapeze. Harcourt, 1964.

The Assyrian, and Other Stories. Harcourt, Brace, 1950.

The Beautiful People. Harcourt, 1941.

Best Stories of William Saroyan. Faber, 1942.

The Bicycle Rider in Beverly Hills. Scribner's, 1952.

Boys and Girls Together. Harcourt, Brace and World, 1963.

The Cave Dwellers; a play. Putnam, 1958.

Chance Meetings. Norton, 1978.

Christmas. Quercus Press, 1939.

A Christmas Psalm. Printed by Grabhorn Press for Gelber, Lilienthal, 1935.

The Daring Young Man on the Flying Trapeze. Random, 1934.

Days of Life and Death and Escape to the Moon. Dial, 1970.

Dear Baby. Harcourt, Brace, 1944.

A Decent Birth, A Happy Funeral; a play in three acts and five scenes. S. French, 1949.

The Dogs, or The Paris Comedy, and Two other Plays; Chris Sick, or Happy New Year Anyway, Making Money, and Nineteen Other Very Short Plays. Phaedra, 1969.

Don't Go Away Mad, and Two Other Plays: Sam Ego's House, and, A Decent Birth, a Happy Funeral. Harcourt, Brace, 1949.

The Fiscal Hoboes. Press of Valenti Angelo, 1949.

Forty-eight Saroyan Stories. Avon, 1942. (Previously published in two books: *Love, Here Is My Hat,* and, *Peace, It's Wonderful.*)

Fragment. Albert M. Bender, 1943.

From Inhale and Exhale, Thirty-one Selected Stories. Avon, 1943.

A Gay and Melancholy Flux. Faber, 1937. (Compiled from *Inhale and Exhale,* and, *Three Times Three.*)

Get Away, Old Man; a play in two acts. Harcourt, Brace, 1944.

Harlem as Seen by Hirschfield. Hyperion Press, 1941.

Hello Out There; a one-act play. S. French, 1949.

Here Comes, There Goes, You Know Who. Simon & Schuster, 1961.

Hilltop Russians in San Francisco. Delkin, 1941. (Pictures by Pauline Vinson; text by William Saroyan.)

Horsey Gorsey and the Frog. E. M. Hale, 1968.

The Human Comedy. Harcourt, Brace, 1943.

The Hungerers; a short play. S. French, 1939.

I Used To Believe I Had Forever, Now I'm Not So Sure. Cowles, 1968.

Inhale and Exhale. Random, 1936.

The Insurance Salesman and Other Stories. Faber & Faber, 1941.

Jim Dandy, Fat Man in a Famine; a play. Harcourt, Brace, 1947.

The Laughing Matter. Doubleday, 1953.

Letters from 74 Rue Taitbout, or, Don't Go, But If You Must, Say Hello to Everybody. World, 1969.

Little Children. Harcourt, 1937.

Look at Us; Let's See; Here We Are; Look Hard, Speak Soft; I See, You See, We All See; Stop, Look, Listen; Beholder's Eye; Don't Look Now, But Isn't That You? (us? U.S.?) Cowles Educational Corporation, 1967. (Photos by Arthur Rothstein.)

Love. Lion Library Editions, 1955.

Love, Here Is My Hat, and Other Short Romances. Modern Age Books, 1938.

Love's Old Sweet Song. S. French, 1941.

Mama, I Love You. Little, 1956.

The Man with the Heart in the Highlands, and Other Stories. Dell, 1968.

Me. Crowell-Collier, 1963. (For younger readers.)

Morris Hirshfield. Rizzoli International, 1976.

My Heart's in the Highlands. Harcourt, 1939.

My Name is Aram. Harcourt, Brace, 1940.

A Native American. George Fields, 1938.

Not Dying. Harcourt, Brace and World, 1963. ("An autobiographical interlude," with drawings by the author.)

Obituaries. Creative Arts, 1979.

Once Around The Block; a play in one act. S. French, 1959.

One Day in the Afternoon of the World. Harcourt, 1964.

Papa, You're Crazy. Little, 1957.

Peace, It's Wonderful. Modern Age Books, 1939.

The Ping-pong Game; a play in one act. S. French, 1940.

Places Where I've Done Time. Praeger, 1972.

Razzle-Dazzle; or, "The human ballet, opera, and circus; or, "There's something I got to tell you: being many kinds of short plays as well as the story of the writing of them." Harcourt, Brace, 1942.

Rock Wagram; a novel. Doubleday, 1951.

Sam Ego's House; a play in three acts and seven scenes. S. French, 1949.

Sam, the Highest Jumper of Them All, or, The London Comedy. Faber, 1961.

Saroyan Fables. Harcourt, Brace, 1941.

The Saroyan Special. Harcourt, 1948.

A Secret Story. Popular Library, 1959. (Originally published as *The Laughing Matter.*)

Settled Out of Court; a play in three acts. S. French, 1962.

Short Drive, Sweet Chariot. Phaedra, 1966.

The Slaughter of the Innocents; a play in two acts. S. French, 1958.

"Some Day I'll Be a Millionaire;" thirty-four more great stories. Avon, 1944.

Sons Come and Go: Mothers Hang in Forever. McGraw-Hill, 1976.

A Special Announcement. House of Books, 1940.

Subway Circus. S. French, 1940.

Thirty-one Selected Stories. Avon, 1943.

Those Who Write Them and Those Who Collect Them. Black Archer Press, 1936.

Three Fragments and a Story. Little Man, 1939.

Three Plays. Harcourt, 1940. (Includes *My Heart's in the Highlands, The Time of Your Life,* and, *Love's Old Sweet Song.*)

Three Plays. Harcourt, 1941. (Includes *The Beautiful People, Sweeney in the Trees,* and, *Across the Board on Tomorrow Morning.*)

Three Times Three. Conference Press, 1936.

The Time of Your Life. Harcourt, 1939.

The Tooth, and, My Father. Doubleday, 1974.

Tracy's Tiger. Doubleday, 1951.

The Trouble with Tigers. Harcourt, Brace, 1938.

The Twin Adventures; The adventures of William Saroyan, a diary. The adventures of Wesley Jackson, a novel. Harcourt, Brace, 1950.

The Whole Voyald, and Other Stories. Little, Brown, 1956.

Why Abstract? Falcon Press, 1948. (Co-authors, Hilaire Hiler and Henry Miller.)

The William Saroyan Reader. Braziller, 1958.

GEORGE STERLING

After Sunset. J. Howell, 1939.

Beyond the Breakers, and Other Poems. A. M. Robertson, 1914.

The Binding of the Beast, and Other War Verse. A. M. Robertson, 1917.

The Caged Eagle, and Other Poems. A. M. Robertson, 1916.

The Evanescent City. A. M. Robertson, 1915.

George Sterling; a centenary memoir-anthology. A. S. Barnes, for the Poetry Society of America, 1969.

The House of Orchids, and Other Poems. A. M. Robertson, 1911.

Lilith; a dramatic poem. A. M. Robertson, 1919.

Ode on the Opening of the Panama-Pacific International Exposition, San Francisco, February 1915. A. M. Robertson, 1915.

Poems to Vera. Oxford University Press, 1938.

Robinson Jeffers; the man and the artist. Boni & Liveright, 1926.

Rosamund; a dramatic poem. A. M. Robertson, 1920.

Sails and Mirage, and Other Poems. A. M. Robertson, 1921.

Selected Poems. Holt, 1923.

Sonnets to Craig. A. & C. Boni, 1928. (Introduction by Upton Sinclair.)

Strange Waters. P. Elder, 1926.

The Testimony of the Suns, and Other Poems. W. E. Wood, 1903.

The Testimony of the Suns; including comments, suggestions, and annotations by Ambrose Bierce . . . together with an introduction by Oscar Lewis. Printed for the Book Club of California by John Henry Nash, 1927.

Thirty-five Sonnets. Book Club of California, 1917.

The Triumph of Bohemia; a forest play. Being the Thirtieth annual midsummer high jinks of the Bohemian Club of San Francisco, as enacted by members of the club at the Bohemian Grove in Sonoma County, California . . . Bohemian Club, 1907.

Truth. The Bookfellows, 1923.

A Wine of Wizardry, and Other Poems. A. M. Robertson, 1909.

Yosemite; an ode. A. M. Robertson, 1916.

ROBERT LOUIS STEVENSON

Across the Plains; with other memories and essays. Chatto & Windus, 1892.

AES Triplex. Scribner's, 1901.

AES Triplex, and Other Essays. T. B. Mosher, 1902.

The Amateur Emigrant; from the Clyde to Sandy Hook. Stone & Kimball, 1895.

Amateur Emigrant; Across the Plains; Silverado Squatters. Scribner's, 1905.

The Beach of Falesá. Heritage Press, 1956.

Black Arrow; a tale of two roses. Cassell, 1888.

The Castaways of Scotland. Private printing, 1928.

Catriona; a sequel to *Kidnapped,* being memoirs of the further adventures of David Balfour at home and abroad. Written by himself and now set forth by Robert Louis Stevenson. Cassell, 1893. (Generally published under the title *David Balfour,* especially in the United States.)

A Child's Garden of Verses. Scribner's, 1895.

A Christmas Sermon. Scribner's, 1900.

Collected Poems. Harte-Davis, 1950.

Complete Poems. Scribner's, 1905.

The Complete Short Stories of Robert Louis Stevenson; with a selection of the best novels. Doubleday, 1969.

David Balfour; being memoirs of the further adventures of David Balfour at home and abroad. Written by himself and now set forth by Robert Louis Stevenson. Scribner's, 1895. (Sometimes published under the title *Catriona.*)

The Dynamiter; more new Arabian nights. Longmans, Green, 1885.

The Ebb-tide; a trio and quartette. Stone & Kimball, 1894.

Edinburgh; picturesque notes. Seeley, Jackson & Halliday, 1879.

The Essay on Walt Whitman. The Roycroft Shop, 1900.

Essays by Robert Louis Stevenson. Scribner's, 1918.

Essays of Travel, and, In the Art of Writing. Scribner's, 1905.

Fables. Scribner's, 1916.

Familiar Studies of Men and Books. Scribner's, 1895.

Father Damien; an open letter to Doctor Hyde of Honolulu, from Robert Louis Stevenson. T. B. Mosher, 1898.

A Footnote to History; eight years of trouble in Samoa. Cassell, 1892.

From Scotland to Silverado; The Amateur Emigrant, from the Clyde to Sandy Hook; Across the Plains; The Silverado Squatters; and Four Essays on California. Harvard University Press, 1966. (Edited by James D. Hart.)

The Great Short Stories of Robert Louis Stevenson. Washington Square Press, 1961.

In the South Seas; being an account of experiences and observations in the Marquesas, Paumotus and Gilbert Islands in the course of two cruises, on the yacht *Casco* (1888) and the schooner *Equator* (1889) by Robert Louis Stevenson. Scribner's, 1905.

An Inland Voyage; an account of the author's canoe trip from Antwerp in Belgium to Pontoise in France. Roberts Brothers, 1905.

Island Nights' Entertainment; The Beach of Falesá; The Bottle Imp; The Isle of Voices. Scribner's, 1893.

Kidnapped; being memoirs of the adventures of David Balfour in the year 1751 . . . written by himself, and now set forth by Robert Louis Stevenson. Scribner's, 1886.

Lay Morals, and Other Papers. Scribner's, 1911.

Learning to Write; suggestions and counsel from Robert Louis Stevenson. Scribner's, 1920.

The Letters of Robert Louis Stevenson to His Family and Friends. Methuen, 1899. (Edited by Sidney Colvin.)

A Lodging for the Night; being a tale concerning one of life's lesser hardships — commonly called trouble. The Roycrofters, 1902.

Master of Ballantrae; a winter's tale. Cassell, 1891.

Memoir of Fleeming Jenkin. Scribner's, 1887.

Memories and Portraits. Scribner's, 1895.

The Merry Men, and Other Tales and Fables; Strange Case of Dr. Jekyll and Mr. Hyde. Scribner's, 1905.

The Mind of Robert Louis Stevenson; selected essays, letters, and prayers. T. Yoseloff, 1963. (Edited by Roger Ricklefs.)

Moral Emblems and Other Poems. Scribner's, 1921.

More New Arabian Nights. Scribner's, 1895.

A Mountain Town in France; a fragment. Lane, 1896. (Includes five illustrations by the author.)

New Arabian Nights. Scribner's, 1896.

New Poems and Variant Readings. Chatto & Windus, 1918.

The Novels and Tales of Robert Louis Stevenson. Scribner's, 1895-1919. 20 volumes.

Our Samoan Adventure. Harper, 1955. (Includes a three-year diary kept by Mrs. Stevenson with rare photos from family albums.)

Poems and Ballads. Scribner's, 1896.

The Poems of Robert Louis Stevenson. Crowell, 1900.

Prayers Written at Vailima. Scribner's, 1904.

Prince Otto; a romance. Scribner's, 1902.

Records of a Family of Engineers. Chatto & Windus, 1912.

R. L. S., An Omnibus. Cassell, 1950. (Selected and edited by G. B. Stern.)

R. L. S.: Stevenson's Letters to Charles Baxter. Yale University Press, 1956.

R. L. Stevenson: The Fabulous Raconteur. Juniper Press, 1959. (Edited by Arno Eckberg.)

Robert Louis Stevenson Hitherto Unpublished Prose Writings. The Robert Louis Stevenson Bibliophile Society, 1921.

Robert Louis Stevenson's Story of Monterey: The Old Pacific Capital. Colt Press, 1944.

St. Ives; being the adventures of a French prisoner in England. Heinemann, 1898.

San Francisco, a Modern Cosmopolis. Book Club of California, 1963. (Preface by James D. Hart.)

The Sea-fogs. P. Elder, 1907.

Selected Poetry and Prose of Robert Louis Stevenson. Houghton Mifflin, 1968. (Edited by Bradford A. Booth.)

Selected Writings of Robert Louis Stevenson. Random, 1947.

The Short Stories of Robert Louis Stevenson. Scribner's, 1923.

The Silverado Squatters. Chatto & Windus, 1883.

Sketches, Criticisms, etc. Scribner's, 1898.

Songs of Travel and Other Verses. Chatto & Windus, 1896.

Stevensoniana; being a reprint of various literary and pictorial miscellany associated with Robert Louis Stevenson, the man and his work. M. F. Mansfield, 1900.

The Strange Case of Dr. Jekyll and Mr. Hyde. Longmans, Green, 1886.

The Suicide Club, and Other Stories. Penguin Books, 1963. (First published as *New Arabian Nights.*)

Tales and Essays. Falcon Press, 1950. (Edited and with an introduction by G. B. Stern.)

The Touchstone; a fable. Greenwillow Books, 1976. (For younger readers.)

Travels in Hawaii. University of Hawaii Press, 1973.

Travels with a Donkey in the Cevennes. Scribner's, 1905.

Treasure Island. Scribner's, 1883.

Underwoods; poems. Scribner's, 1887.

Vailima Letters; being correspondence addressed by Robert Louis Stevenson to Sidney Colvin, November 1890-October 1894. Stone & Kimball, 1895. 2 volumes.

"Virginibus Puerisque," and Other Papers. C. K. Paul, 1881.

Weir of Hermiston; an unfinished romance. Chatto & Windus, 1896.

When the Devil Was Well; hitherto unpublished story. Bibliophile Society, 1921.

Will O' the Mill. The Roycroft Shop, 1901.

The Works of Robert Louis Stevenson. Longmans Green, 1894-1898. 28 volumes.

The Wrecker. Scribner's, 1892. (Co-author, Lloyd Osbourne.)

The Wrong Box. Longmans, Green, 1889. (Co-author, Lloyd Osbourne.)

GEORGE R. STEWART

American Given Names: Their Origin and History in the Context of the English Language. Oxford University Press, 1979.

American Place Names: A Concise and Selective Dictionary for the Continental United States of America. Oxford University Press, 1970.

American Ways of Life. Doubleday, 1954.

A Bibliography of the Writings of Bret Harte in the Magazines and Newspapers of California, 1857-1871. University of California Press, 1933.

Bret Harte, Argonaut and Exile; being an account of the life of the celebrated American humorist, author of "The Luck of Roaring Camp," "Condensed Novels," "The Heathen Chinee," "Tales of the Argonauts," etc., etc., compiled from new and original sources. Houghton Mifflin, 1931.

The California Trail: An Epic With Many Heroes. McGraw-Hill, 1962.

Committee of Vigilance: Revolution in San Francisco, 1851; an account of the hundred days when certain citizens undertook the suppression of the criminal activities of the Sydney ducks. Houghton Mifflin, 1964.

The Department of English of the University of California on the Berkeley Campus; an informal presentation of some of its personalities and activities during its first century. University of California, 1968.

Doctor's Oral. Random, 1939.

Donner Pass and Those Who Crossed It; the story of the country made notable by the Stevens Party, the Donner Party, the gold-hunters, and the railway builders. California Historical Society, 1960.

Earth Abides. Random, 1949.

East of the Giants; a novel. Holt, 1938.

English Composition; a laboratory course. Holt, 1936.

Fire; a novel. Random, 1948.

Good Lives. Houghton Mifflin, 1967.

John Phoenix, Esq., the Veritable Squibob; a life of Captain George H. Derby, U.S.A. Holt, 1937.

Man; an autobiography. Random, 1946.

N.A. 1: the North-South Continental Highway. Houghton Mifflin, 1957. 2 volumes.

Names on the Globe. Oxford University Press, 1975.

Names on the Land; a historical account of place-naming in the United States. Random, 1945.

Not So Rich As You Think. Houghton Mifflin, 1968.

Ordeal By Hunger; the story of the Donner Party. Holt, 1936.

Pickett's Charge; a microhistory of the final attack at Gettysburg, July 3, 1863. Houghton Mifflin, 1959.

Sheep Rock; a novel. Random, 1951.

Storm; a novel. Random, 1941.

Take Your Bible in One Hand; the life of William Henry Thomes. Colt Press, 1939.

The Techniques of English Verse. Holt, 1930.

This California. Diable Press, 1965. (Text by George Stewart; photos by Michael Bry.)

To California By Covered Wagon. Random, 1964. (For younger readers.)

U.S. 40: Cross Section of the United States of America. Houghton Mifflin, 1953.

The Year of the Oath; the fight for academic freedom at the University of California, written in collaboration with other professors of the University of California. Doubleday, 1950.

The Years of the City. Houghton Mifflin, 1955.

MARK TWAIN

The Adventures of Colonel Sellers. Being Mark Twain's share of *The Gilded Age,* a novel which he wrote with Charles Dudley Warner. Now published separately for the first time and comprising, in effect, a new work. Doubleday, 1965. (Edited, with notes and introduction, by Charles Neider.)

The Adventures of Huckleberry Finn (Tom Sawyer's Comrade). Webster, 1885.

The Adventures of Thomas Jefferson Snodgrass. P. Covici, 1928.

The Adventures of Tom Sawyer. American Publishing Company, 1876.

Ah, Sin, a dramatic work by Mark Twain and Bret Harte. Book Club of California, 1961. (Edited by Frederick Anderson.)

The American Claimant. Webster, 1892.

The Art, Humor, and Humanity of Mark Twain. University of Oklahoma Press, 1959.

The Birds and Beasts of Mark Twain. University of Oklahoma Press, 1966.

A Book For An Hour, containing choice reading and character sketches. A curious dream, and other sketches. 1873.

Celebrated Jumping Frog of Calaveras County, and other sketches. C. H. Webb, 1867.

Christian Science, with notes concerning corrections to date. Harper, 1907.

The Christmas Fireside. The story of a bad little boy that bore a charmed life. Written by Grandfather Twain for good little girls and boys. L-D Allen Press, 1949.

Clemens of the Call: Mark Twain in San Francisco. University of California Press, 1969. (Edited by Edgar M. Branch.)

The Comic Mark Twain Reader: the most humorous selections from his stories, sketches, novels, travel books, and lectures. Doubleday, 1977.

Complete Essays of Mark Twain, now collected for the first time. Doubleday, 1963. (Edited and with an introduction by Charles Neider.)

Complete Humorous Sketches and Tales of Mark Twain, now collected for the first time. Doubleday, 1961. (Edited and with an introduction by Charles Neider.)

Complete Short Stories of Mark Twain, now collected for the first time. Doubleday, 1957. (Edited and with an introduction by Charles Neider.)

Complete Travel Books of Mark Twain. Doubleday, 1966-1967. 2 volumes. (Edited and with an introduction by Charles Neider.)

Concerning Cats; two tales. Book Club of California, 1959. (Edited by Frederick Anderson.)

A Connecticut Yankee in King Arthur's Court. Webster, 1889.

Contributions to the Galaxy, 1868-1871. Scholars' Facsimiles and Reprints, 1961.

The Curious Republic of Gondour; and other whimsical sketches. Boni & Liveright, 1919.

Date 1601; conversation as it was by the social fireside in the time of the Tudors. West Point, 1882.

The Devil's Race-Track: Mark Twain's Great Dark Writings. University of California Press, 1980. (Edited by John S. Tuckey.)

The Diaries of Adam and Eve. American Heritage Press, 1971.

A Dog's Tale. Harper, 1904.

A Double Barrelled Detective Story. Harper, 1902.

Early Tales and Sketches. University of California Press, 1979.

Editorial Wild Oats. Harper, 1905.

Edmund Burke on Croker and Tammany. Economist Press, 1901.

English As She Is Taught. Mutual Book Company, 1900.

Europe and Elsewhere. Harper, 1923.

Everyone's Mark Twain. A. S. Barnes, 1972. (Edited by Caroline Thomas Harnsberger.)

Eve's Diary; translated from the original manuscript by Mark Twain. Harper, 1906.

Extract from Captain Stormfield's Visit to Heaven. Harper, 1909.

Extracts from Adam's Diary; translated from the original manuscript. Harper, 1904.

Fables of Man. University of California Press, 1972.

Following the Equator; a journey around the world. American Publishing Company, 1897.

The Forgotten Writings of Mark Twain. Philosophical Library, 1963.

Gilded Age: A Tale of To-Day. American Publishing Company, 1873-1874. (Co-author, Charles Dudley Warner.)

A Horse's Tale. Harper, 1907.

How to Tell a Story, and other essays. Harper, 1897.

In Defense of Harriet Shelley, and other essays. Harper, 1918.

The Innocents Abroad; or, The new Pilgrim's Progress: being some account of the steamship Quaker City's pleasure excursion to Europe and the Holy Land. . . . American Publishing Company, 1869.

The Innocents at Home. Tauchnitz, 1881.

Is Shakespeare Dead? From my autobiography. Harper, 1909.

King Leopold's Soliloquy; a defense of his Congo rule. P. R. Warner, 1905.

Letters from Honolulu, written for the *Sacramento Union.* T. Nickerson, 1939.

Letters from the Earth. Harper, 1962. (Edited by Bernard DeVoto.)

Letters from the Sandwich Islands, written for the *Sacramento Union.* Stanford University Press, 1938.

The Letters of Quintus Curtius Snodgrass. Southern Methodist University, 1946.

Life As I Find It. Essays, sketches, tales, and other material, the majority of which is now published in book form for the first time. Hanover House, 1961. (Edited, with introduction and notes, by Charles Neider.)

Life on the Mississippi. Osgood, 1883.

Literary Essays. Harper, 1899. (Also published under the title *How To Tell a Story.*)

The Love Letters of Mark Twain. Harper, 1949.

The Mammoth Cod, and, Address to the Stomach Club. Maledicta, 1976.

The Man That Corrupted Hadleyburg, and other essays and stories. Harper, 1900.

Mark Twain and the Government. Caxton Printers, 1960.

Mark Twain and the Three R's: race, religion, revolution — and related matters. Bobbs-Merrill, 1973.

Mark Twain, Business Man. Little, Brown, 1946.

Mark Twain-Howells Letters; the correspondence of Samuel L. Clemens and William Dean Howells, 1872-1910.

Belknap Press of Harvard University, 1960. (Edited by Henry Nash Smith and William M. Gibson.)

Mark Twain in Eruption: hitherto unpublished pages about men and events. Harper, 1940. (Edited by Bernard DeVoto.)

Mark Twain of the Enterprise; newspaper articles and other documents, 1862-1864. University of California Press, 1957. (Edited by Henry Nash Smith and Frederick Anderson.)

Mark Twain on the Damned Human Race. Hill and Wang, 1962.

Mark Twain: San Francisco Correspondent; selections from his letters to the *Territorial Enterprise:* 1865-1866. Book Club of California, 1957. (Edited by Henry Nash Smith and Frederick Anderson.)

Mark Twain, the Letter Writer. Meador Publishing Company, 1932.

Mark Twain to Mrs. Fairbanks. Huntington Library, 1949. (Edited by Dixon Wecter.)

Mark Twain's Autobiography. Harper, 1924. 2 volumes.

Mark Twain's (Burlesque) Autobiography and First Romance. Sheldon, 1871.

Mark Twain's Correspondence with Henry Huttleston Rogers, 1893-1909. University of California Press, 1969. (Edited by Lewis Leary.)

Mark Twain's Hannibal, Huck, and Tom. University of California Press, 1969. (Edited by Walter Blair.)

Mark Twain's Letter to the California Pioneers. DeWitt & Snelling, 1911.

Mark Twain's Letters. Harper, 1917. 2 volumes.

Mark Twain's Letters from Hawaii. Appleton-Century, 1966. (Edited by A. Grove Day.)

Mark Twain's Letters in the Muscatine Journal. The Mark Twain Association of America, 1942.

Mark Twain's Letters to His Publishers, 1867-1894. University of California Press, 1967. (Edited with an introduction by Hamlin Hill.)

Mark Twain's Letters to Mary. Columbia University Press, 1961.

Mark Twain's Letters to Will Bowen, "my first, & oldest & dearest friend." University of Texas, 1941.

Mark Twain's Library of Humor. Webster, 1888.

Mark Twain's Mysterious Stranger Manuscripts. University of California Press, 1969. (Edited by William M. Gibson.)

Mark Twain's Notebook. Harper, 1923.

Mark Twain's Notebook and Journals. University of California Press, 1976-79. 3 volumes. (Edited by Frederick Anderson, *et al.*)

Mark Twain's San Francisco, McGraw-Hill, 1963.

Mark Twain's Satires and Burlesques. University of California Press, 1967. (Edited by Franklin R. Rogers.)

Mark Twain's Speeches. Harper, 1910. (Introduction by William Dean Howells.)

Mark Twain's Travels with Mr. Brown. Knopf, 1940.

Mark Twain's "Which Was the Dream?" and other symbolic writings of the later years. University of California Press, 1966. (Edited by John S. Tuckey.)

Merry Tales. Webster, 1892.

Moments with Mark Twain. Harper, 1920. (Selected by Albert Bigelow Paine.)

More Tramps Abroad. Tauchnitz, 1897. (Previously published as *Following the Equator.*)

My Debut as a Literary Person, with other essays and stories. American Publishing Company, 1903.

The Mysterious Stranger; a romance. Harper, 1916.

Old Times on the Mississippi. Rose-Belford, 1878.

The $1,000,000 Bank-Note, and other new stories. Webster, 1893.

A Pen Warmed-up in Hell: Mark Twain in Protest. Harper & Row, 1972.

Personal Recollections of Joan of Arc. Harper, 1896.

The Portable Mark Twain. Viking, 1946. (Edited by Bernard DeVoto.)

Practical Jokes with Artemus Ward. J. C. Hotten, 1874.

The Prince and the Pauper; a tale for young people of all ages. Osgood, 1882.

Punch, Brothers, Punch! and other sketches. Slote, Woodman, 1878.

The Quaker City Holy Land Excursion; an unfinished play. Privately printed, 1927.

Rambling Notes of an Idle Excursion. Rose-Belford, 1878.

Report from Paradise. Harper, 1952.

Republican Letters. International Mark Twain Society, 1941. (Edited by Cyril Clemens; foreword by Sir Hugh Walpole.)

Roughing It. American Publishing Company, 1872.

Saint Joan of Arc. Harper, 1919.

Screamers; a gathering of scraps of humor, delicious bits, and short stories. J. C. Hotten, 1871.

Simon Wheeler, Detective. New York Public Library, 1963.

1601; or, A Fireside Conversation in Ye Time of Queen Elizabeth. Privately printed, 1929. (See *Date 1601.*)

Sketches New and Old. American Publishing Company, 1875.

Sketches of the Sixties; being forgotten material now collected for the first time from the *Californian, 1864-1867.* J. Howell, 1926. (Co-author, Bret Harte.)

Stolen White Elephant, etc. Osgood, 1882.

The $30,000 Bequest, and other stories. Harper, 1906.

Tom Sawyer Abroad. By Huck Finn. Webster, 1894.

Tom Sawyer Abroad. Tom Sawyer, Detective; with other stories, etc., etc. Harper, 1896.

The Tragedy of Pudd'nhead Wilson, and, The Comedy, Those Extraordinary Twins. American Publishing Company, 1894.

A Tramp Abroad. American Publishing Company, 1880. 2 volumes.

Traveling with the Innocents Abroad; Mr. Twain's original reports from Europe and the Holy Land. University of Oklahoma Press, 1958.

A True Story, and, The Recent Carnival of Crime. Osgood, 1877.

The Unabridged Mark Twain. Running Press, 1976, 1979. (Opening remarks by Kurt Vonnegut, Jr.) 2 volumes.

Washington in 1868. International Mark Twain Society, 1943.

Washoe Giant in San Francisco, being hitherto unpublished sketches by Mark Twain published in the Golden era in the sixties. . . . G. Fields, 1938.

What Is Man? and other essays. Privately printed, 1906.

Works. (Various editions, including Newbegin, 29 volumes; etc.)

The Writings of Mark Twain. (Various editions, including Harper, 1923-1925, 37 volumes.)

Your Personal Mark Twain, in which the great American ventures an opinion on ladies, language, liberty, literature, liquor, love, and other controversial subjects. International Publishers, 1960.